Rice Cooker Creations
With Debra Murray

ACKNOWLEDGEMENTS

I would like to thank my husband Martin, daughter Nevar, my parents, and the rest of my family for supporting my career and encouraging me to become an author. None of my achievements would have become a reality without the help and guidance of Chef Wolfgang Puck. Thank you for all your support. It is truly an honor and a privilege to be associated with such an outstanding chef and amazing person.

My sincere thanks to Sydney Silverman and Mike Sanseverino, the best people one could ever hope to work for.

Special thanks to Marian Getz, it is a delight to work with you.

I would also like to thank the team behind the book: Jonathan Schwartz for your guidance, Daniel Koren for your creative influence, Chris Davis and his assistants Yildred Tortosa and Erica Taylor for taking breathtaking photographs.

Thanks to Tracy Ferguson for art direction and Christina Chancey for food styling.

Thank you to my loyal HSN viewers who are constantly sharing their passion with me. We often share recipes, and I have included some of them in this book.

This book is dedicated to Suzanne Fitzgerald.

INTRODUCTION

Debra Murray has been my assistant at the Home Shopping Network for almost ten years, and I have witnessed time after time her passion for good cooking and quality appliances to make anyone a better cook. The rice cooker is one of her favorite tools, and I have urged her to share her favorite recipes with as many people as possible through this book.

The rice cooker is one of my favorite appliances, too. Rice may seem like a simple food to prepare, but it can be tricky. During the early days of my culinary career, I never knew if my rice was going to come out dry, soggy, or overcooked. If I had a rice cooker, I would have been able to make perfect rice every time.

Debra Murray knows how to take advantage of the rice cooker. She combines rice with high quality, seasonal, locally grown ingredients to make easy, delicious and effortless meals in no time. The rice cooker makes it possible to enjoy all types of cuisines, even my mother's and grandmother's rice pudding. Most importantly, in this age of two-career couples, where many families find it difficult to put a home-cooked dinner on the table each evening, Debra shows us how the rice cooker can allow us to do just that.

A talented cook in her own right, Debra shares my WELL (Wolfgang's Eat, Love, Live!™) philosophy of good cooking and warm hospitality. I believe everyone should use the freshest, all-natural ingredients, food that is locally grown, organic whenever possible, and raised using sustainable humane methods.

As I learned long ago, alongside my mother and grandmother, you should always put lots of love into everything you cook. This is certainly evident in this collection of Debra Murray's rice cooker recipes.

Wolfgang Puck

TABLE OF CONTENTS

Rice, Grains & Legumes
Page 9

Side Dishes
Page 35

Soups
Page 52

One Pot Pasta Meals
Page 69

TABLE OF CONTENTS

RICE COOKER TIPS

Rice cookers have gained popularity in recent years, not only for their ability to cook perfect rice but also for their versatility and ease of use. You can cook almost anything in a rice cooker: meat, chicken, pork, soups, vegetables, and even desserts. The possibilities are endless.

There are a few rice cooker tips I would like to share with you to help you achieve excellent results:

How to measure rice:

The rice cooker comes with a small plastic measuring cup. It can hold the equivalent of ¾ cup (standard U.S. cup) and is referred to as "a measure". The recipes in this book use standard U.S. cups. If you would like to use your plastic measuring cup, make sure you convert accordingly.

Please note that the line markings inside the rice cooker correspond with the number of measures of rice. For instance, 3 measures of rice will be placed in the rice cooker and liquid will be filled to the corresponding line marking inside the rice cooker. Use this information as a general guideline, as I have included the exact amount of liquid for each recipe throughout this book.

How to rinse rice:

Use a fine strainer or colander when rinsing rice and always rinse after measuring. Certain types of rice should not be rinsed: For instance, Arborio rice as it contains a starch that makes it creamy, or yellow rice which contains seasoning.

Consistency:

For a softer rice consistency, add more water. Deduct water if you like firmer rice.

RICE COOKER TIPS

Recommended types of rice:

White rice, brown rice, basmati rice, jasmine rice, wild rice, and most long or short grain rice cook perfectly in the rice cooker. However, I do not recommend buying the converted box rice or the parboiled rice which are processed and tend to discolor and overcook in the rice cooker.

Rice tips:

Add a teaspoon of salt and a teaspoon of oil to the liquid before cooking. To achieve perfectly fluffed rice, let rice rest on KEEP WARM mode for 15 minutes after cooking and then stir to fluff the rice. Also, keep lid secured to preserve the texture until ready to serve.

Cake tips:

The rice cooker is a perfect tool for cakes as well. The most effective method for making cakes is to press the COOK button every 10 minutes until total cooking time is reached. Always test for doneness with a wooden pick and allow cake to cool with the rice cooker unplugged for at least 30 minutes before inverting onto a cake stand.

Pasta tips:

For every 2 cups of small dry pasta (rotini, elbow macaroni, etc.), use 1½ cups of liquid. You can use stock for more flavor but you can also use water seasoned with a teaspoon of salt and a tablespoon of extra-virgin olive oil. Larger pasta (penne, rigatoni, etc.) require 2 cups of dry pasta to 2 cups of liquid.

Braising tips:

Always make sure there is at least 1½ cups of liquid for every hour you plan on cooking as the rice cooker requires steam to function properly. Never thicken the gravy until the meat is 95% done.

RICE COOKER TIPS

Steaming tips:

Most rice cookers are equipped with a steamer basket. Simply pour ½ cup of water in the rice cooker and load the steamer basket with your favorite fish or vegetables. Every ½ cup of water will allow you to steam for 5 to 7 minutes. If steaming corn or shrimp, increase the liquid by ½ cup and steam for 12 minutes.

Differences between rice cookers:

The recipes in this book can be prepared in any rice cooker. I strongly recommend using a Wolfgang Puck rice cooker. Depending on the size of your rice cooker, some ingredient adjustments may be necessary. The recipes were created using a 7 cup rice cooker. As a general rule, if you have a 5 cup rice cooker, simply reduce the ingredients listed in each recipe by half and follow the cooking instructions. If you have a 10 cup rice cooker, simply double the ingredients and follow the cooking instructions. For your convenience, I have added the conversions for the 5 cup rice cooker to the back of this book. A few other things to remember are not to fill the rice cooker beyond the max line of the rice cooker insert, cooking time may vary depending on your location, your rice cooker model or ingredients used. Also, if the rice cooker switches to KEEP WARM before the suggested cooking time is reached, add additional liquid, ¼ cup at a time and press COOK again.

Wine reduction:

Rice cookers are also great for wine reductions because they will reduce the wine without burning it as the sugar will trigger the rice cooker to go to KEEP WARM.

Sous Vide:

There is a new culinary movement called "Sous Vide" where chefs cook meats low and slow to achieve a tender result with no shrinkage. Typically the food is vacuum sealed and cooked for 24 hours. The internal temperature of the rice cooker on KEEP WARM allows you to cook this way without having to vacuum seal or turn on your big stove.

Rice, Grains & Legumes

DEB'S FAVORITE RICE

Ingredients:

2 cups jasmine or basmati rice

2 cups water

1 teaspoon salt

1 teaspoon extra-virgin olive oil

1. Rinse rice in strainer for 2 minutes until water runs clear.
2. Place all ingredients into rice cooker.
3. Secure lid and press COOK.
4. Cooking is complete when rice cooker switches to KEEP WARM (about 25 minutes).

Deb's Tip:
For more tender rice, add an additional quarter cup of water before cooking.

RICE COOKER JAMBALAYA

By Shannon Dillman   Makes 6 servings

Ingredients:

1 box (8 ounces) New Orleans style jambalaya mix

2½ cups chicken stock

2 tablespoons extra-virgin olive oil

½ pound kielbasa

½ pound shrimp, peeled and deveined

½ pound cooked chicken, white or dark meat

1 can (14½ ounces) tomatoes, chopped

¼ cup onions, chopped

¼ cup green peppers, chopped

1 bag (10 ounces) frozen corn

2 cups black beans, drained

1. Place all ingredients, except shrimp, into rice cooker.
2. Secure lid and press COOK.
3. After 10 minutes of cooking, add shrimp to rice cooker.
4. Cooking is complete when rice cooker switches to KEEP WARM (about 20 minutes).

SUSHI RICE

Ingredients:

2 cups short-grain rice

2 cups water

2 tablespoons rice vinegar

2 tablespoons mirin

1 tablespoon salt

1. Rinse rice.
2. Place all ingredients into rice cooker; stir.
3. Secure lid and press COOK.
4. Cooking is complete when rice cooker switches to KEEP WARM (about 15 minutes).
5. Let rice rest in KEEP WARM for an additional 15 minutes.

GREEN RICE

Ingredients:

1½ cup Arborio rice

2 tablespoons chopped green chiles, canned

1 small green pepper, chopped

1 garlic clove, minced

½ cup fresh cilantro, chopped

1 bunch flat leaf parsley, chopped

1 tablespoon lime juice

1 small onion, minced

2 cups chicken stock

1. Place all ingredients into rice cooker.
2. Secure lid and press COOK.
3. Cooking is complete when rice cooker switches to KEEP WARM (about 25 minutes).

Deb's Tip:
This recipe makes a terrific addition
to a grilled fish dish.

EASY FIESTA RICE

Ingredients:

1 small onion, chopped

2 cans (10 ounces each) diced tomatoes with lime juice and cilantro, drained

2¼ cups long-grain rice

1¼ cup chicken stock

1 teaspoon salt

¼ teaspoon freshly ground pepper

1. Place all ingredients into rice cooker.
2. Secure lid and press COOK.
3. Cooking is complete when rice cooker switches to KEEP WARM (about 20 minutes).

Deb's Tip:
As a variation, add a half cup of drained whole kernel corn.

DEB'S FAVORITE FRIED RICE

Ingredients:

1 tablespoon sesame oil

2 garlic cloves, minced

1 teaspoon freshly grated ginger

½ teaspoon sugar

1 carrot, shredded

4 cups long-grain rice, cooked

½ cup chicken, cut into ½-inch pieces

2 tablespoons soy sauce

1 tablespoon fish sauce

2 tablespoons green onions, chopped

¼ cup bean sprouts

¼ cup peas

2 large eggs, beaten

1. Pour oil into rice cooker and press COOK; heat oil for 5 minutes.
2. Add chicken to rice cooker; cook for 5 minutes.
3. Add ginger, garlic and sugar to rice cooker; cook for 3 minutes.
4. Add remaining ingredients, except eggs and green onions, to rice cooker.
5. Secure lid and press COOK; cook for an additional 5 minutes.
6. Pour eggs into rice cooker while stirring; cook until eggs are done.
7. Garnish with green onions and serve.

Deb's Tip:
Pork is an ideal substitute for chicken in this rice.

BROWN RICE & BARLEY PILAF

Ingredients:

1 cup basmati brown rice

1 cup pearl barley

3 cups chicken stock

1 medium onion, diced

1 apple, peeled and cored

1 sprig of fresh thyme

1 teaspoon fennel seeds

1. Place all ingredients into rice cooker.
2. Secure lid and press COOK.
3. Cooking is complete when rice cooker switches to KEEP WARM (about 40 minutes).

Deb's Tip:
Add broth to this dish and eat it as a soup.

BROWN RICE WITH WHITE MISO

Makes 4 servings

Ingredients:

2 cups long-grain brown rice

4 cups water

1 tablespoon white miso paste

1. Place rice into rice cooker.

2. Secure lid and press COOK; cook rice for 10 minutes until nicely toasted.

3. Add remaining ingredients to rice cooker.

4. Secure lid and press COOK; cook for 45 minutes.

Deb's Tip:
If you feel like enjoying this dish with some vegetables, just load the steamer basket with cauliflower or broccoli during the last 10 minutes of cooking.

SPICY SHRIMP RISOTTO

Ingredients:

1 tablespoon extra-virgin olive oil

1 whole shallot, finely chopped

1 small green pepper, finely chopped

2 garlic cloves, minced

2 tablespoons tomato paste

1 teaspoon salt

1 teaspoon freshly ground pepper

1 cup Arborio rice

½ cup dry white wine

2 cups chicken stock

1 bay leaf

⅓ teaspoon crushed red pepper flakes

1 pound large shrimp, peeled and deveined

½ cup Romano cheese, shredded

3 basil leaves, torn

1. Press COOK and let rice cooker preheat for 5 minutes.
2. Add shallots and oil to rice cooker; cook for 4 minutes.
3. Add green peppers and garlic to rice cooker.
4. Secure lid and press COOK; cook for 3 minutes.
5. Add rice and tomato paste to rice cooker; cook for an additional 5 minutes.
6. Add wine, 1½ cups stock, bay leaf, salt and pepper.
7. Secure lid and press COOK; cook for 15 minutes.
8. Add shrimp, red pepper flakes and ½ cup stock; stir.
9. Secure lid and press COOK; cook for 15 minutes.
10. Add cheese to rice cooker; stir.
11. Garnish with fresh basil and serve.

RISOTTO WITH ASPARAGUS

Ingredients:

1½ cups Arborio rice

8 ounces fresh asparagus, peeled, cut into 1-inch pieces

1 small onion, chopped

2 tablespoons salted butter, melted

½ teaspoon salt

½ teaspoon freshly ground pepper

2½ cups chicken stock

¾ cup Parmesan cheese, grated

1. Rinse and drain rice.
2. Place butter and onions into rice cooker.
3. Secure lid and press COOK; cook for 4 minutes.
4. Add remaining ingredients, except Parmesan, to rice cooker; stir.
5. Secure lid and press COOK.
6. When rice cooker switches to KEEP WARM (about 20 minutes), add Parmesan to rice cooker; stir and serve.

CUBAN STYLE BLACK BEANS

Makes 6 to 8 servings

Ingredients:

1 bag (12 ounces) black beans

2 envelopes Spanish seasoning

4 cups beef stock

1 medium onion, diced

1 red bell pepper, chopped

1 tablespoon cilantro, chopped

2 ripe plum tomatoes, chopped

1 garlic clove, minced

1 can (10½ ounces) diced tomatoes with green chiles and lime

1. Sort and wash beans.
2. Place beans into rice cooker, cover with water and add Spanish seasoning.
3. Let soak for 2 hours.
4. Add remaining ingredients.
5. Secure lid and press COOK; cook for 2 hours; stir occasionally.
6. If rice cooker switches to KEEP WARM during the 2 hours, add ½ cup of stock, stir and press COOK again.
7. Cooking is complete when rice cooker switches to KEEP WARM.

RED BEANS & RICE

Ingredients:

2¼ cups long-grain rice

1 cup red beans, canned or cooked, drained

1 medium celery, chopped

1 small onion, chopped

2 garlic cloves, minced

½ cup ham, diced

½ cup smoked sausage, sliced

2 cups beef stock

1 teaspoon hot sauce

1 teaspoon Worcestershire sauce

½ cup tomato sauce

1 teaspoon prepared mustard

1 whole bay leaf

1 teaspoon Cajun spice

1. Place all ingredients into rice cooker.
2. Secure lid and press COOK.
3. Cooking is complete when rice cooker switches to KEEP WARM (about 20 minutes).

NEW ENGLAND BAKED BEANS

Ingredients:

1 pound navy beans

6 ounces salt pork, cut into 1-inch pieces

1 medium onion, chopped

4 cups water

½ teaspoon baking soda

½ cup sugar

¼ cup molasses

1 tablespoon prepared mustard

1 tablespoon salt

¼ cup maple syrup

1 tablespoon Jamaican pepper sauce

1 slice fresh ginger

1. Sort and wash beans.
2. Place beans into a bowl and cover with water; let soak overnight.
3. The next day, rinse and drain beans.
4. Press COOK and let rice cooker preheat for 5 minutes.
5. Place pork into rice cooker and cook for 3 minutes.
6. Add onions to rice cooker, press COOK and cook for 2 minutes.
7. Add beans to rice cooker.
8. Pour 4 cups of water into rice cooker and add remaining ingredients.
9. Secure lid and press COOK; cook for 2 hours.
10. After 1½ hours, check if beans are moist; if necessary add ½ cup of water and press COOK again.
11. Cooking is complete when rice cooker switches to KEEP WARM.

Deb's Tip:
For a twist, add a half cup of diced, red bell peppers.

QUINOA PILAF

Ingredients:

1 tablespoon extra-virgin olive oil

4 ounces mushrooms, sliced

1 teaspoon salt

½ teaspoon freshly ground pepper

½ cup onions, finely chopped

1½ cups quinoa

2 cups chicken stock

1. Pour oil into rice cooker and press COOK; heat oil for 5 minutes.
2. Add mushrooms, onions, salt and pepper to rice cooker.
3. Secure lid and press COOK; cook for 5 minutes.
4. Using a fine strainer, rinse quinoa.
5. Add quinoa and stock to rice cooker; stir.
6. Secure lid and press COOK; cook for 20 minutes.
7. Stir to fluff quinoa.
8. Secure lid and set rice cooker to KEEP WARM; cook for 10 minutes.

Deb's Tip:
For a sweeter taste, add fresh tarragon to this dish.

HUMMUS

Ingredients:

2 cups dry garbanzo beans

7 cups water

4 whole garlic cloves

6 cups chicken stock

3 tablespoons tahini

2 tablespoons fresh lemon juice

1 tablespoon extra-virgin olive oil

¼ teaspoon cayenne pepper

2 teaspoons salt

1. Sort and wash beans.
2. Place beans into a bowl and cover with water; let soak overnight.
3. The next day, rinse and drain beans.
4. Place beans, garlic and stock into rice cooker.
5. Secure lid and press COOK.
6. Cook until rice cooker switches to KEEP WARM (about 2 hours).
7. Drain beans.
8. Place beans and remaining ingredients into a food processor; blend until smooth.
9. Serve with flat bread or warm pitas.

Deb's Tip:
For a different flavor, add a quarter cup of sun-dried tomatoes or roasted red peppers.

ITALIAN POLENTA

Makes 6 servings

Ingredients:

4 cups water

1 cup coarse grain yellow polenta

1 teaspoon salt

½ teaspoon freshly ground pepper

⅓ cup unsalted butter

½ cup Parmesan cheese, grated

1. Place polenta, water, salt and pepper into rice cooker; stir until lump-free.
2. Secure lid and press COOK; cook for 15 minutes; stir.
3. Secure lid and cook for an additional 15 minutes.
4. Add butter and cheese to rice cooker; stir.

Deb's Tip:
As a variation, spray a bowl with non-stick spray, pour the polenta into the bowl and let it set for 10 minutes; invert polenta onto a platter and serve with tomato sauce and cheese.

OLD FASHIONED STEEL CUT OATS

Ingredients:

2½ cups water or apple cider

¼ teaspoon salt

1 cup steel oats

1 cinnamon stick

1. Place all ingredients into rice cooker.
2. Secure lid and press COOK.
3. Cooking is complete when rice cooker switches to KEEP WARM (about 20 minutes).
4. Serve hot with milk or cream.

Deb's Tip:
For a sweeter taste, add some honey or maple syrup.

GRITS

By Josephine Cook   Makes 6 to 8 servings

Ingredients:

1 cup grits, not quick-cook

4½ cups cold water

1 tablespoon salted butter

1. In a bowl, combine all ingredients; mix well.
2. Pour mixture into rice cooker.
3. Secure lid and press COOK.
4. Cooking is complete when rice cooker switches to KEEP WARM (about 25 minutes).

Josephine's Tip:
For a cheesy alternative, add shredded Parmesan or Cheddar cheese to the grits after it is done cooking.

Side Dishes

GARLIC MASHED POTATOES

Ingredients:

6 Yukon gold potatoes, peeled and cut in half

1½ cups chicken stock

½ cup heavy cream

3 whole garlic cloves

1 teaspoon salt

½ teaspoon freshly ground pepper

1. Place all ingredients into rice cooker.
2. Secure lid and press COOK; cook for 20 minutes.
3. Smash potatoes with potato masher.
4. Taste for additional salt and pepper.

OLD FASHIONED POTATO SALAD

Ingredients:

3 large eggs

½ cup water

½ teaspoon salt

¼ teaspoon freshly ground pepper

1 tablespoon kosher dill pickle juice

1 teaspoon celery seed

2 pounds Russet potatoes, peeled, cut into 2-inch cubes

½ teaspoon celery salt

1 medium onion, chopped

2 celery stalks, chopped

1 tablespoon prepared mustard

½ cup mayonnaise

1. Place potatoes and water into rice cooker.
2. Sprinkle with salt and pepper.
3. Gently place eggs on top of the potatoes.
4. Secure lid and press COOK; cook for 20 minutes.
5. Transfer eggs to a bowl of cold water.
6. Transfer potatoes to another bowl.
7. Drizzle potatoes with pickle juice; season with celery salt and seed.
8. Cover and refrigerate for one hour.
9. Peel and chop eggs.
10. Combine potatoes, eggs, mayonnaise, onions, celery and mustard.
11. Mix well.

Deb's Tip:
If you do not like pickle juice, substitute with vinegar.

SCALLOPED POTATOES WITH CHEDDAR CHEESE

Ingredients:

2 tablespoons unsalted butter

1 medium onion, thinly sliced

2 garlic cloves, minced

2½ pounds Russet potatoes, peeled, sliced ⅛-inch thick

1 tablespoon fresh thyme leaves

1 teaspoon kosher salt

½ teaspoon freshly ground pepper

½ cup chicken stock

½ cup heavy cream

Pinch of nutmeg

4 ounces Cheddar cheese, shredded

2 tablespoons fresh chives, chopped

1. Place butter into rice cooker and press COOK.
2. When butter is melted, add onions and sauté for 4 minutes.
3. Add garlic, potatoes, salt, pepper, thyme and stock to rice cooker.
4. Secure lid and press COOK; cook for 15 minutes.
5. Add remaining ingredients and stir.
6. Secure lid and press COOK.
7. Cooking is complete when rice cooker switches to KEEP WARM (about 10 minutes).
8. Let rest in KEEP WARM for 10 minutes before serving.
9. Garnish with chives.

GERMAN POTATO SALAD

Makes 8 servings

Ingredients:

2 pounds small red potatoes

2½ cups water

3 teaspoons salt

½ pound bacon, cut into ½-inch pieces

¼ cup flour

½ cup cider vinegar

1½ tablespoons sugar

¼ teaspoon freshly ground pepper

½ cup onions, chopped

1 teaspoon celery seed

1. Place potatoes, 1 cup of water and 1 teaspoon of salt into rice cooker.
2. Secure lid and press COOK; cook for 20 minutes.
3. Transfer potatoes to a plate and clean rice cooker.
4. Peel and slice potatoes.
5. Place bacon into rice cooker, secure lid and press COOK.
6. Cook bacon for 5 minutes until crisp; transfer bacon to a plate.
7. Add flour to remaining bacon grease inside rice cooker; stir until smooth.
8. Add 1½ cups of water, vinegar, sugar, 2 teaspoons of salt, pepper and celery seed.
9. Press COOK and continue to stir until mixture comes to a boil.
10. Secure lid and cook for an additional 5 minutes; stir.
11. Add onions, potatoes and bacon to rice cooker; stir.
12. Secure lid and press COOK.
13. Cooking is complete when rice cooker switches to KEEP WARM.

Deb's Tip:
Garnish with a handful of crisp bacon.

41

FLAVORFUL SMASHED POTATOES

Ingredients:

6 Russet potatoes, peeled and quartered

1 tablespoon extra-virgin olive oil

2 whole garlic cloves

1 rutabaga, peeled, cut into 2-inch pieces

½ teaspoon salt

1 teaspoon freshly ground pepper

3 tablespoons salted butter

1 tablespoon cream or milk

1. Pour oil into rice cooker and press COOK; heat oil for 5 minutes.
2. Add garlic to rice cooker and sauté for 2 minutes; do not brown.
3. Add potatoes, rutabaga and stock to rice cooker.
4. Secure lid and press COOK; cook for 30 minutes.
5. Add remaining ingredients to rice cooker; stir.
6. Using a potato masher, smash potatoes until slightly chunky.

Deb's Tip:
If you don't have rutabaga handy, just use celery root, parsnips or turnips.

CREAMED CORN

Ingredients:

3 tablespoons salted butter

½ cup onions, diced

1 pound frozen corn kernels

½ cup chicken stock

1 teaspoon salt

½ teaspoon freshly ground pepper

½ teaspoon sugar

3 ounces cream cheese

½ cup heavy cream

1. Place butter into rice cooker.
2. Secure lid and press COOK; cook for 5 minutes.
3. Add onions; cook for an additional 5 minutes.
4. Add corn, stock, sugar, salt and pepper to rice cooker.
5. Secure lid and press COOK; cook for 25 minutes.
6. Add cream cheese and cream to rice cooker.
7. Secure lid and press COOK; cook for an additional 5 minutes.
8. Purée with an Immersion blender for desired consistency.

Deb's Tip:
For a southwestern twist, add 2 tablespoons of chopped green chiles.

GREEN BEANS WITH TOMATOES

Ingredients:

1 pound fresh green beans, washed and trimmed

1 tablespoon extra-virgin olive oil

1 medium sweet onion, thinly sliced

1 pint grape tomatoes, diced

½ cup chicken stock

1 teaspoon salt

½ teaspoon freshly ground pepper

6 basil leaves, torn

1. Pour oil into rice cooker and press COOK; heat oil for 5 minutes.

2. Add onions to rice cooker; cook for 5 minutes.

3. Add remaining ingredients, except basil, to rice cooker.

4. Secure lid and press COOK; cook for 15 minutes.

5. Add basil to rice cooker, stir and cook for an additional 5 minutes.

Deb's Tip:
For extra flavor, top the beans with a quarter cup of crumbled feta cheese.

BACON & SWEET ONION GREEN BEANS

Ingredients:

3 strips of bacon, cut into 1-inch pieces

1 medium onion, chopped

1 pound pole beans, trimmed, cut into 1-inch pieces

¼ cup water

1 teaspoon salt

½ teaspoon freshly ground pepper

1. Press COOK and let rice cooker preheat for 5 minutes.
2. Place bacon into rice cooker and cook for 5 minutes.
3. Add onions to rice cooker and cook for an additional 3 minutes.
4. Place remaining ingredients into rice cooker; stir.
5. Secure lid and press COOK; cook for 15 minutes.

OYSTER CASSEROLE

Makes 4 servings

Ingredients:

1 tablespoon extra-virgin olive oil

1 medium onion, chopped

1 celery stalk, finely chopped

3 tablespoons fresh parsley, chopped

1 package (10 ounces) frozen spinach

1 teaspoon salt

1 tablespoon Worcestershire sauce

1 tablespoon salted butter

2 cups cracker crumbs

1 pint oysters with juice

½ cup Parmesan cheese, shredded

1. Pour oil into rice cooker and press COOK; heat oil for 5 minutes.
2. Add onions and celery to rice cooker; cook for 5 minutes.
3. Add remaining ingredients to rice cooker; stir.
4. Secure lid and press COOK; cook for 30 minutes.
5. Rice cooker will switch to KEEP WARM multiple times during the 30 minutes, press COOK every 10 minutes.

EGGPLANT LASAGNA

Ingredients:

1 large eggplant, sliced into ¼-inch rounds

2 large eggs, beaten

3 tablespoons extra-virgin olive oil

2 cups whole milk Ricotta cheese

¼ cup Parmesan cheese, shredded

1 teaspoon salt

1 teaspoon freshly ground pepper

1 jar (26 ounces) pasta sauce

1 pound Mozzarella cheese, shredded

6 basil leaves, torn

1. In a sauté pan, heat 1 inch of oil over medium heat for 8 minutes.
2. Dip eggplant slices into eggs and place into pan; brown on both sides.
3. Remove from oil and pat dry.
4. In a bowl, combine Ricotta, Parmesan, basil, salt and pepper; mix well.
5. Pour 1 cup of pasta sauce into rice cooker and cover with 1 layer of eggplant slices.
6. Add ½ of the Ricotta mixture and ⅓ of the Mozzarella.
7. Top with 1 cup of pasta sauce and 1 additional layer of eggplant slices.
8. Add remaining Ricotta mixture and ⅓ of the Mozzarella.
9. Top with 1 cup of pasta sauce, remaining eggplant slices, sauce and Mozzarella.
10. Secure lid and press COOK; cook for 20 minutes.
11. Let cool for 20 minutes before serving.

BONNIE'S CHEESY RICE & VEGGIES

By Bonnie Davis   Makes 6 to 8 servings

Ingredients:

2 cups basmati or long-grain rice

2¼ cups chicken stock

1 medium onion, finely chopped

1 celery stalk, sliced

1 bag (16 ounces) frozen broccoli

1 bag (16 ounces) frozen cauliflower

1 can (10¾ ounces) cream of mushroom soup

1 jar (8 ounces) pasteurized process cheese sauce

½ cup milk

¼ cup salted butter

1. Place rice, stock, celery and onions into rice cooker.
2. Secure lid and press COOK; cook for 20 minutes.
3. Add remaining ingredients to rice cooker.
4. Secure lid and press COOK.
5. Cook until rice cooker switches to KEEP WARM (about 8 minutes); stir.
6. Secure lid and press COOK again.
7. Cooking is complete when rice cooker switches to KEEP WARM.
8. Let rest for 10 minutes before serving.

CAULIFLOWER PUREE

Ingredients:

1 large head of cauliflower, sliced into 1-inch pieces

1 teaspoon salt

½ teaspoon freshly ground pepper

1 cup chicken stock

4 ounces cream cheese

2 tablespoons salted butter

1. Place cauliflower, stock, salt and pepper into rice cooker.
2. Secure lid and press COOK; cook for 25 minutes until cauliflower is tender; drain.
3. Using an Immersion blender, purée cauliflower with cream cheese and butter.

Deb's Tip:
This recipe is a great alternative to potatoes as it has half the calories and half the carbohydrates.

Soups

GREEK LEMON CHICKEN SOUP

Ingredients:

3 boneless, skinless chicken breasts, diced into 1-inch cubes

1 medium onion, chopped

1 cup fresh spinach, chopped

6 cups chicken stock

½ cup orzo pasta

4 tablespoons fresh lemon juice

1 teaspoon kosher salt

1 teaspoon freshly ground pepper

1 tablespoon fresh mint leaves, chopped

2 large eggs, beaten

1. Place all ingredients, except eggs and mint leaves, into rice cooker.
2. Secure lid and press COOK; cook for 30 minutes.
3. Pour eggs into rice cooker while stirring.
4. Sprinkle with mint leaves and serve.

Deb's Tip:
For a gluten-free alternative,
substitute Arborio rice for the orzo.

VEGETABLE SOUP WITH PASTA

Ingredients:

1 cup onions, chopped

1 tablespoon extra-virgin olive oil

1 garlic clove, minced

1 cup celery, sliced

1 cup carrots, sliced

1 cup cabbage, sliced

1 can (14½ ounces) diced tomatoes with oregano and garlic

4 cups vegetable stock

1 sprig fresh thyme

1 cup dry wagon wheel pasta

1. Place oil and onions into rice cooker.
2. Secure lid and press COOK; cook for 5 minutes.
3. Add remaining ingredients, except pasta, to rice cooker.
4. Secure lid and press COOK; cook for 25 minutes.
5. Add pasta to rice cooker and cook for an additional 10 minutes.

CLAM CHOWDER

Ingredients:

25 steamer or Littleneck clams

1 cup water

1 medium onion, chopped

1 celery root, peeled, cut into 1-inch pieces

½ teaspoon freshly ground pepper

4 ounces salt pork, rind removed, cut into ¼-inch pieces

1 sprig of fresh thyme

1 teaspoon salt

2 cups chicken stock

1 cup cream

Fresh parsley, chopped

1. Place clams and water into rice cooker.
2. Secure lid and press COOK; cook for 15 minutes.
3. Strain clams through a fine strainer, reserving the broth.
4. Clams should all be open; discard unopened clams.
5. Add pork to rice cooker.
6. Secure lid and press COOK; cook for 5 minutes.
7. Add onions to rice cooker and cook for an additional 4 minutes.
8. Add celery root, stock, clam broth, thyme, salt and pepper.
9. Secure lid and press COOK; cook for 20 minutes.
10. Remove thyme.
11. Add cream and clams. Shuck the clams or serve them in the shell.
12. Secure lid and press COOK; cook for an additional 5 minutes.
13. Sprinkle with parsley and serve.

Deb's Tip:
As a variation, add 1 cup of fresh corn to this dish.

SPLIT PEA SOUP

Ingredients:

2 cups dried split peas

1 cup ham, diced

3 carrots, cut into 2-inch pieces

1 medium onion, diced

3 celery stalks, cut into 1-inch pieces

2 garlic cloves, minced

1 bay leaf

1 sprig of fresh thyme

6 cups chicken stock

½ teaspoon freshly ground pepper

1. Place all ingredients into rice cooker.
2. Secure lid and press COOK; cook for 45 minutes.
3. If softer consistency is desired, add another cup of stock and press COOK again.
4. Cook until peas are tender.

Deb's Tip:
For extra flavor, add a ham bone to the soup while it is cooking.

THAI STYLE CHICKEN SOUP

Ingredients:

1 tablespoon extra-virgin olive oil

1 small purple onion, thinly sliced

1 small red pepper, julienned

2 garlic cloves, minced

1 teaspoon freshly grated ginger

1 can (6 ounces) bamboo shoots

2 tablespoons creamy peanut butter

2 tablespoons brown sugar

2 cups cooked chicken, shredded

1 can (13½ ounces) coconut milk

2 cups chicken stock

1 teaspoon Chinese five-spice powder

1 tablespoon fish sauce

1 lemon, juice and zest

2 tablespoons green onions, chopped

2 tablespoons cilantro, chopped

1. Press COOK and let rice cooker preheat for 5 minutes.
2. Add oil and onions to rice cooker; sauté for 5 minutes.
3. Add peppers, ginger and garlic; cook for an additional 2 minutes.
4. Add bamboo shoots, peanut butter and sugar to rice cooker; stir.
5. Add remaining ingredients to rice cooker; stir.
6. Secure lid and press COOK; cook for 20 minutes.
7. Garnish with green onions and cilantro.

BORSCHT

Ingredients:

1 tablespoon extra-virgin olive oil

1 medium onion, diced

½ cup carrots, diced

½ cup celery, sliced

½ cup cabbage, shredded

1 cup potatoes, diced

2 cups beef stock

2 cups beets, peeled and diced

1 can (14½ ounces) petite diced tomatoes

1 teaspoon cider vinegar

1 teaspoon salt

½ teaspoon freshly ground pepper

Sour cream

8 sprigs of fresh dill

1. Pour oil into rice cooker and press COOK; heat oil for 5 minutes.
2. Add onions to rice cooker; cook for 3 minutes.
3. Add remaining ingredients, except sour cream and dill, to rice cooker.
4. Secure lid and press COOK; cook for 30 minutes.
5. Purée the soup with an Immersion blender until smooth.
6. Serve with a dollop of sour cream and a sprig of fresh dill.

ALMOST HOMEMADE CHICKEN SOUP

Ingredients:

2 boneless, skinless frozen chicken breasts

6 cups chicken stock

1 sprig of fresh thyme

½ cup carrots, sliced 1-inch thick

1 small onion, diced

1 teaspoon salt

1 teaspoon freshly ground pepper

½ cup wide egg noodles

1 tablespoon fresh parsley, chopped

1. Place all ingredients, except noodles and parsley, into rice cooker.
2. Secure lid and press COOK; cook for 45 minutes.
3. Using a skimmer, remove foam from top of the soup.
4. Remove chicken and thyme from rice cooker.
5. Cut chicken into small pieces and return to rice cooker.
6. Add noodles to rice cooker.
7. Secure lid and press COOK; cook for 15 minutes.
8. Set rice cooker to KEEP WARM and add parsley; stir.
9. Taste for additional salt and pepper.

Deb's Tip:
For a fancy twist, substitute tortellini for the egg noodles.

BUTTERNUT SQUASH-APPLE SOUP

Makes 6 to 8 servings

Ingredients:

1 tablespoon extra-virgin olive oil

1 medium onion, chopped

1 medium butternut squash, peeled and seeded

2 Granny Smith apples, peeled and cored

3 cups chicken stock

2 cups apple cider

1 sprig of fresh thyme

1 sprig of rosemary

2 sage leaves

½ cup cream

Sour cream

1. Press COOK and let rice cooker preheat for 5 minutes.
2. Add oil and onions to rice cooker.
3. Secure lid and press COOK.
4. When rice cooker switches to KEEP WARM, add remaining ingredients, except cream.
5. Secure lid and press COOK; cook for 30 minutes.
6. Remove herbs from rice cooker.
7. Using an Immersion blender, add cream to rice cooker and purée until smooth.
8. Garnish with sour cream and serve.

Deb's Tip:
Serve this soup in espresso cups
as a first course.

ROASTED RED PEPPER SOUP

Ingredients:

2 tablespoons extra-virgin olive oil

5 garlic cloves, chopped

1 large onion, chopped

1 cup celery, chopped

1 cup carrots, chopped

2 tablespoons tomato paste

1 jar (24 ounces) roasted red peppers, drained

6 cups vegetable stock

1 bay leaf

1 teaspoon salt

½ teaspoon freshly ground pepper

Fresh basil, chopped

Sour cream

1. Pour oil into rice cooker and press COOK; heat oil for 5 minutes.
2. Add onions, celery and carrots to rice cooker; cook for 5 minutes.
3. Add garlic and tomato paste to rice cooker; cook for 2 minutes.
4. Add bay leaf, stock and peppers to rice cooker.
5. Secure lid and press COOK; cook for 15 minutes.
6. Remove bay leaf and purée using an Immersion blender.
7. Garnish with sour cream and basil.

BEEF BARLEY SOUP

Ingredients:

1 to 1½ pounds beef shanks, bone-in

1 tablespoon extra-virgin olive oil

2 cups dry red wine

1 teaspoon salt

½ teaspoon freshly ground pepper

1 small onion, quartered

4 cups beef stock

3 large carrots, sliced

1 large celery stalk, sliced

1 medium onion, thinly sliced

1 can (14½ ounces) petite diced tomatoes

1 sprig of fresh thyme

1 bay leaf

½ cup pearl barley

1. Pour oil into rice cooker and press COOK; heat oil for 5 minutes.
2. Add beef to rice cooker and brown on both sides.
3. Add wine, quartered onions, salt and pepper to rice cooker.
4. Secure lid and press COOK; cook for 1½ hours.
5. Remove beef from rice cooker; trim fat and cut meat into small pieces.
6. Place meat and remaining ingredients into rice cooker.
7. Secure lid and press COOK; cook for 35 minutes.
8. Taste for additional salt and pepper.

Deb's Tip:
For extra flavor, add 1 pound of bones to the rice cooker
that have been roasted in the oven for 1 hour.

One Pot Pasta Meals

CREAMY ONE POT MACARONI & CHEESE

Ingredients:

2 cups elbow macaroni

1½ cups chicken stock

1 teaspoon salt

½ teaspoon freshly ground pepper

1 cup cream

1½ cups mild Cheddar cheese, shredded

½ cup Mozzarella cheese, shredded

2 tablespoons salted butter

Pinch of nutmeg

1. Place macaroni, stock, salt and pepper into rice cooker.
2. Secure lid and press COOK.
3. Cook until rice cooker switches to KEEP WARM (about 15 minutes).
4. Add remaining ingredients to rice cooker; stir.
5. Secure lid and press COOK; cook for an additional 5 minutes.

CHICKEN FETTUCCINE ALFREDO

Makes 4 servings

Ingredients:

2 boneless, skinless frozen chicken breasts

3 cups chicken stock

8 ounces fettuccine nests, uncooked

1 teaspoon salt

1 teaspoon freshly ground pepper

2 garlic cloves, minced

4 ounces cream cheese

½ cup cream

½ cup Parmesan and Romano cheese mix, shredded

1 tablespoon fresh parsley, chopped

1. Place chicken, stock, garlic, salt and pepper into rice cooker.
2. Secure lid and press COOK; cook for 25 minutes.
3. Remove chicken from rice cooker and chop into 1-inch pieces.
4. Place fettuccine into rice cooker and top with chopped chicken.
5. Secure lid and press COOK; cook for 10 minutes; stir.
6. Add cream cheese and cream to rice cooker.
7. Secure lid and press COOK; cook for an additional 5 minutes.
8. Add cheese mix and parsley to rice cooker; stir well and serve.

Deb's Tip:
For even more flavor, add sauteed mushrooms or chopped artichoke hearts to this dish.

LINGUINI & LENTILS

By Josephine Cook

Ingredients:

1 package (15½ ounces) lentils

1 tablespoon extra-virgin olive oil

2 garlic cloves, minced

1 large onion, chopped

1 carrot, chopped

10 cups water

¼ cup tomato sauce

1½ teaspoons salt

1 teaspoon freshly ground pepper

½ teaspoon crushed red pepper flakes

6 ounces dry linguini nests

1. Sort and wash lentils.
2. Place garlic, onions, carrots and oil into rice cooker.
3. Secure lid and press COOK; cook for 3 minutes.
4. Add lentils, 8 cups of water, salt, pepper, tomato sauce and red pepper flakes to rice cooker; stir.
5. Secure lid and press COOK; cook for 35 minutes.
6. Add remaining 2 cups of water to rice cooker.
7. Secure lid and press COOK; cook for an additional 10 minutes.
8. Cooking is complete when linguini is al dente.

Josephine's Tip:
Serve with a nice crusty bread.

ORZO WITH SUN-DRIED TOMATOES & SPINACH

Ingredients:

1 cup orzo

1 cup chicken stock

2 tablespoons sun-dried tomato pesto

½ cup fresh spinach, chopped

8 basil leaves, chopped

1. Place all ingredients into rice cooker.
2. Secure lid and press COOK.
3. When rice cooker switches to KEEP WARM (about 13 minutes), stir and let rest on KEEP WARM for 5 minutes before serving.

Deb's Tip:
This dish is delicious served with lamb chops.

BAKED ZITI

Makes 4 to 6 servings

Ingredients:

1 pound ground beef

1 small onion, chopped

2 garlic cloves, minced

1 teaspoon salt

½ teaspoon freshly ground pepper

2 cups dry ziti pasta

1½ cups beef stock

1 jar (26 ounces) pasta sauce

2 cups whole milk Ricotta cheese

2 cups Mozzarella cheese, shredded

½ cup Parmesan cheese, shredded

1. Crumble ground beef and place into rice cooker.
2. Secure lid and press COOK.
3. Cook until rice cooker switches to KEEP WARM; drain fat.
4. Add onions, garlic, salt and pepper to rice cooker.
5. Secure lid and press COOK; cook for 5 minutes.
6. Add pasta, stock and sauce to rice cooker.
7. Secure lid and press COOK.
8. When rice cooker switches to KEEP WARM (about 15 minutes), add Ricotta, Parmesan and Mozzarella to rice cooker; stir.
9. Secure lid and press COOK.
10. Cooking is complete when rice cooker switches to KEEP WARM (about 5 minutes).

PASTA PRIMAVERA

Makes 2 to 4 servings

Ingredients:

2 cups dry ziti or penne

2 cups beef stock

1½ cups pasta sauce

1 cup fresh mixed vegetables, sliced

¼ cup Mozzarella cheese, shredded

1. Place pasta, stock and sauce into rice cooker.
2. Secure lid and press COOK; cook for 10 minutes.
3. Add vegetables to rice cooker; stir.
4. Sprinkle with cheese.
5. Secure lid and press COOK; cook for an additional 3 minutes.

Deb's Tip:
You can substitute the fresh vegetables with a
bag of mixed frozen vegetables.

PASTA FAGIOLI

By Josephine Cook   Makes 8 servings

Ingredients:

3 garlic cloves, minced

1 stick (6½ ounces) pepperoni, skin removed, cut into ½-inch pieces

1 tablespoon extra-virgin olive oil

1 can (19 ounces) cannellini beans

1 can (8 ounces) tomato sauce

6 cups water

½ teaspoon freshly ground pepper

1 teaspoon salt

¼ teaspoon crushed red pepper flakes

2 cups ditalini pasta

1. Place pepperoni, garlic and oil into rice cooker.
2. Secure lid and press COOK; cook for 3 minutes.
3. Add beans, salt, pepper, tomato sauce, 1 cup of water and red pepper flakes to rice cooker; stir.
4. Secure lid and press COOK; cook for 5 minutes.
5. Add pasta and remaining water to rice cooker; stir.
6. Secure lid and press COOK; cook for 30 minutes.
7. Cooking is complete when pasta is done but not mushy.

Josephine's Tip:
Serve with a nice crusty bread.

ORECCHIETTE WITH BROCCOLI & SAUSAGE

Ingredients:

1 pound Italian turkey sausage, casings removed

4 garlic cloves, sliced

2 cups orecchiette pasta

3 cups chicken stock

2 cups broccoli flowerets

¼ teaspoon crushed red pepper flakes

1 cup Parmesan cheese, shredded

Fresh parsley, chopped

1. Place sausage into rice cooker and crumble using a rubber spatula.
2. Secure lid and press COOK; cook for 5 minutes; drain fat.
3. Add garlic to rice cooker and cook for an additional 3 minutes.
4. Add pasta and 1½ cups stock to rice cooker.
5. Secure lid and press COOK.
6. Cook until rice cooker switches to KEEP WARM (about 15 minutes).
7. Add remaining stock, broccoli and cheese.
8. Secure lid and press COOK; cook for an additional 5 minutes.
9. Toss with red pepper flakes and garnish with freshly chopped parsley.

PAD THAI

Ingredients:

2 garlic cloves, minced

1 teaspoon sesame oil

2 boxes Pad Thai stir-fry rice noodles with sauce

4 cups water

2 tablespoons lime juice

1 cup bean sprouts

1 pound medium shrimp, peeled and deveined

3 green onions, cut into 1-inch pieces

1 tablespoon fresh cilantro, chopped

½ cup peanuts

½ teaspoon crushed red pepper flakes

1. Pour oil into rice cooker and press COOK; heat oil for 5 minutes.
2. Add garlic to rice cooker and sauté for 2 minutes.
3. Add water, sauce and lime juice to rice cooker.
4. Secure lid and press COOK; cook for 10 minutes.
5. Add remaining ingredients to rice cooker.
6. Secure lid and press COOK; cook for an additional 5 minutes.

Deb's Tip:
For more flavor, substitute 1 cup of light coconut milk
for 1 cup of water.

SPAGHETTI PIE

Ingredients:

2 large eggs, beaten

1 tablespoon extra-virgin olive oil

1 teaspoon Italian herbs

½ cup Parmesan cheese, shredded

1 pound spaghetti, cooked

¾ cup pasta or meat sauce

½ cup Mozzarella cheese, shredded

2 tablespoons fresh parsley, chopped

Non-stick cooking spray

1. In a bowl, combine eggs, Italian herbs, salt and pepper; mix well.
2. Add oil, Parmesan and spaghetti to bowl; toss well.
3. Spray rice cooker with non-stick spray.
4. Pour spaghetti mixture into rice cooker; top with sauce and Mozzarella.
5. Secure lid and press COOK.
6. Cook until rice cooker switches to KEEP WARM (about 5 minutes).
7. Wait 10 minutes and press COOK again.
8. Cooking is complete when rice cooker switches to KEEP WARM (about 5 minutes).

PASTA BOWS WITH PROSCIUTTO & PEAS

Makes 2 to 4 servings

Ingredients:

1 tablespoon extra-virgin olive oil

3 garlic cloves, minced

4 ounces prosciutto, chopped into ¼-inch pieces

2 cups dry bow tie pasta

1½ cups chicken stock

1½ cups tiny peas

½ cup dry white wine

½ cup cream

½ teaspoon salt

½ teaspoon freshly ground pepper

5 mint or basil leaves, chopped

1. Pour oil into rice cooker and press COOK; heat oil for 5 minutes.
2. Add garlic and prosciutto to rice cooker; cook for 3 minutes.
3. Add pasta and stock to rice cooker.
4. Secure lid and press COOK.
5. Cook until rice cooker switches to KEEP WARM (about 15 minutes).
6. Add wine, peas, cream, salt and pepper to rice cooker; stir.
7. Secure lid and press COOK; cook for an additional 5 minutes.
8. Garnish with mint or basil and serve.

TUSCAN SHRIMP PASTA

Makes 4 to 6 servings

Ingredients:

2 cups dry ziti or penne

1½ cups chicken stock

1 small purple onion, thinly sliced

2 garlic cloves, minced

1 can (14 ounces) artichoke heats, drained and quartered

¼ cup sun-dried tomatoes, oil-packed

1 pound shrimp, peeled and deveined

¼ cup Kalamata olives

½ cup fresh pesto

1. Place pasta, stock, onions and garlic into rice cooker.
2. Fit rice cooker with steamer basket and place shrimp into basket.
3. Secure lid and press COOK.
4. When rice cooker switches to KEEP WARM, remove steamer basket.
5. Add shrimp and remaining ingredients to rice cooker; toss well.
6. Serve hot or cold.

PASTA IN A PINCH

Ingredients:

2 cups dry penne pasta

2 cups chicken stock

1 jar (28 ounces) pasta sauce

¼ cup Parmesan cheese, shredded

½ cup mushrooms

1. Place all ingredients into rice cooker.
2. Secure lid and press COOK.
3. Cook until rice cooker switches to KEEP WARM (about 20 minutes); stir.
4. Let cook on KEEP WARM for an additional 5 minutes.

Beef

POT ROAST

By Josephine Cook   Makes 4 servings

Ingredients:

1½ to 2 pound pot roast

½ cup flour

2 large yellow onions, thinly sliced

3½ cups beef stock

1 stick salted butter

1. Cut roast into chunks and coat with flour.
2. Add butter to rice cooker and press COOK.
3. When butter is melted, place roast into rice cooker; brown on all sides.
4. Add onions and stock.
5. Secure lid and press COOK; cook for 3 hours until meat is tender.
6. If rice cooker switches to KEEP WARM during the 3 hours, add ¼ cup of water and press COOK again.
7. Cooking is complete when rice cooker switches to KEEP WARM.
8. Serve with mashed potatoes.

Josephine's Tip:
To make this meal even more delicious, place some baby carrots in the steamer basket during the last 20 minutes of cooking.

BEEF BURRITOS

Ingredients:

1 tablespoon extra-virgin olive oil

1 medium onion, diced

2 garlic cloves, minced

1 pound flank steak, cut in half

2 cups beef stock

1 envelope taco seasoning

½ teaspoon cumin

1 can (10½ ounces) diced tomatoes with green chiles, mild

6 flour tortillas

1 cup Mexican cheese, shredded

Green onions, chopped

Sour cream

1. Pour oil into rice cooker and press COOK; heat oil for 5 minutes.
2. Add onions to rice cooker; cook for 3 minutes.
3. Add garlic and steak to rice cooker; brown on both sides.
4. Add stock, seasoning, tomatoes and cumin to rice cooker.
5. Secure lid and press COOK; cook for 90 minutes.
6. Shred steak with a fork.
7. If meat is not falling apart, add ½ cup of stock and cook for an additional 30 minutes.
8. Place meat in the center of each tortilla and roll into a burrito.
9. Garnish with sour cream and green onions.

STUFFED PEPPERS

Ingredients:

1 pound ground beef

1 medium onion, chopped

4 bell peppers

1 cup rice, cooked

1 can (14½ ounces) diced tomatoes with basil, garlic and oregano

1 teaspoon salt

½ teaspoon freshly ground pepper

2 cups pasta sauce

4 slices Swiss cheese

1. Press COOK and let rice cooker preheat for 5 minutes.
2. Crumble beef and place into rice cooker; secure lid and press COOK.
3. When rice cooker switches to KEEP WARM, drain fat.
4. Add onions, salt and pepper to rice cooker; cook for 5 minutes.
5. Cut off pepper tops; remove membranes and seeds.
6. In a bowl, combine ground beef, rice and diced tomatoes.
7. Divide meat mixture between peppers.
8. Place stuffed peppers into rice cooker and top each pepper with 1 slice of cheese.
9. Pour pasta sauce over peppers.
10. Secure lid and press COOK.
11. Cooking is complete when rice cooker switches to KEEP WARM (about 30 minutes).

Deb's Tip:
For a variation, you can use turkey, chicken or pork to stuff the peppers.

RICE COOKER MEATBALLS

Ingredients:

1 tablespoon extra-virgin olive oil

1 small onion, minced

3 garlic cloves, minced

2 pounds lean ground beef

¾ cup bread crumbs, finely grated

½ cup beef stock

½ cup Parmesan cheese, grated

1 teaspoon garlic salt

½ teaspoon freshly ground pepper

2 large eggs, beaten

4 cups tomato sauce

1. Pour oil into rice cooker and press COOK; heat oil for 5 minutes.
2. Add onions and garlic to rice cooker.
3. Secure lid and press COOK; cook for 5 minutes.
4. Transfer onions and garlic to a large bowl; let cool.
5. Add bread crumbs and stock to bowl; let soak.
6. Add remaining ingredients, except tomato sauce, to bowl; stir.
7. Shape mixture into even-sized meatballs; place into rice cooker.
8. Pour tomato sauce into rice cooker.
9. Secure lid and press COOK; cook for 25 minutes.
10. Skim excess fat before serving.

CORNED BEEF & CABBAGE

Ingredients:

2 pound corned beef brisket, cut in half

1 bottle (12 ounces) dark beer

2 cups beef stock

4 garlic cloves, minced

2 medium onions, quartered

2 tablespoons pickling spice

4 medium red potatoes, halved

1 large cabbage head, cut into wedges

1 cup baby carrots

1. Rinse beef and trim excess fat.
2. Place beef, beer, stock and pickling spice into rice cooker.
3. Secure lid and press COOK; cook for 4 hours.
4. Place remaining ingredients on top of beef; add ½ cup of water if water has evaporated.
5. Secure lid and press COOK; cook for 15 minutes.
6. Serve with spicy mustard.

SLOPPY JOES

By Christina Chancey   Makes 6 to 8 servings

Ingredients:

2 pounds lean ground beef

1 small onion, chopped

2 garlic cloves, minced

½ green bell pepper, chopped

3 tablespoons Worcestershire sauce

3 tablespoons brown sugar

2 teaspoons yellow mustard

2 teaspoons cider vinegar

1½ teaspoons chili powder

1 can (6 ounces) tomato paste

1 cup water

1. Place all ingredients, except beef, into rice cooker; stir.
2. Crumble beef over mixture; stir.
3. Secure lid and press COOK;
4. Cook until rice cooker switches to KEEP WARM (about 20 minutes).
5. Stir well and press COOK again; cook for an additional 5 minutes.
6. Stir well and serve.

Chicken

CHICKEN ENCHILADA CASSEROLE

Ingredients:

2 cups cooked chicken

1 can (4½ ounces) chopped green chiles

1 package taco seasoning

1 cup chicken stock

1 can (19 ounces) tortilla soup

Tortilla chips

1 can (10 ounces) enchilada sauce

1 cup mild Cheddar cheese, shredded

3 green onions, chopped

Sour cream

1. Place chicken, chiles, seasoning, stock and soup into rice cooker.
2. Secure lid and press COOK; cook for 15 minutes.
3. Top chicken with tortillas, enchilada sauce and cheddar.
4. Secure lid and press COOK; cook for an additional 10 minutes.
5. Sprinkle with green onions and serve with sour cream.

Deb's Tip:
Substitute frozen chicken tenders for cooked chicken and add 15 minutes to the cooking time.

CHICKEN CACCIATORE

By D'Ann Mathews   Makes 6 servings

Ingredients:

8 boneless, skinless frozen chicken tenderloins

Pinch of garlic and herb seasoning

Pinch of Italian seasoning

1 teaspoon sugar

1 cup onions, thinly sliced

½ cup red wine

1 cup mushrooms, thinly sliced

1½ cups spaghetti sauce

1 cup four-cheese mix, shredded

1. Spray rice cooker with non-stick spray.
2. Place 4 tenderloins into rice cooker and sprinkle with seasonings.
3. Top tenderloins with ½ cup onions and ½ cup mushrooms.
4. In a bowl, combine spaghetti sauce and red wine.
5. Pour half of the red wine mixture over chicken.
6. Repeat layering with remaining chicken, seasonings, onions and mushrooms.
7. Sprinkle with sugar and pour remaining red wine mixture over chicken.
8. Secure lid and press COOK; cook for 35 minutes.
9. Open lid and sprinkle cheese over chicken.
10. Secure lid and set rice cooker to KEEP WARM; cook for 5 minutes until cheese is melted.
11. Serve over pasta.

CHICKEN & YELLOW RICE WITH PEAS

Makes 6 servings

Ingredients:

2¼ cups yellow rice

1 cup cooked chicken

2 tablespoons extra-virgin olive oil

1 small onion, chopped

1 garlic clove, minced

1 small red pepper, cut into strips

1 cup frozen peas

2 tablespoons stuffed green olives, sliced

2¼ cups chicken stock

1. Rinse and drain rice.
2. Place all ingredients into rice cooker.
3. Secure lid and press COOK.
4. Cooking is complete when rice cooker switches to KEEP WARM (about 25 minutes).

Deb's Tip:
To spice this up, add a couple slices of chorizo sausage.

ASIAN CHICKEN WITH RICE NOODLES

Ingredients:

1 tablespoon sesame oil

8 ounces boneless, skinless chicken breast or thigh, cut into ½-inch pieces

½ teaspoon Chinese five-spice powder

1 garlic clove, minced

1 teaspoon freshly grated ginger

½ teaspoon chili pepper paste

3 tablespoons stir-fry sauce

1 teaspoon rice wine vinegar or mirin

1 can (14 ounces) stir-fry vegetables, drained

3 ounces rice sticks (Py Mai Fun)

2 tablespoons green onions, chopped

1. Pour oil into rice cooker and press COOK; heat oil for 5 minutes.
2. Rub chicken with five-spice powder and place into rice cooker.
3. Secure lid and press COOK; cook for 5 minutes.
4. In a bowl, soak rice sticks in 3 cups of warm water for 20 minutes.
5. Add garlic, ginger and chili paste to rice cooker; stir and cook for 2 minutes.
6. Add stir-fry sauce, vinegar and vegetables to rice cooker; stir.
7. Secure lid and press COOK; cook for 20 minutes.
8. Drain rice sticks and transfer to rice cooker; stir.
9. Secure lid and press COOK; cook for an additional 5 minutes.
10. Garnish with green onions.

Deb's Tip:
To transform this dish to a tasty stir-fry over steaming rice, add 2 cups of fresh vegetables like pea pods or broccoli after step 7 and cook for an additional 5 minutes; serve with steaming rice.

CHICKEN CURRY

Ingredients:

1 tablespoon extra-virgin olive oil

2 chicken breasts, cubed

½ cup orange juice or maple syrup

1½ tablespoons curry powder

1 cup peas

½ cup red bell peppers, diced

½ cup orange bell peppers, diced

½ cup yellow bell peppers, diced

½ cup mushrooms, sliced

1. Pour oil into rice cooker and press COOK; heat oil for 5 minutes.
2. Add chicken to rice cooker; brown on all sides.
3. Add remaining ingredients to rice cooker.
4. Secure lid and press COOK; cook for 20 minutes.
5. Serve over rice.

CHICKEN & DUMPLINGS

Ingredients:

8 medium chicken thighs or legs, skinless

1 teaspoon salt

Pinch of poultry seasoning

½ teaspoon freshly ground pepper

1 teaspoon extra-virgin olive oil

1 cup onions, sliced

1 cup celery, diced

1 can (10¾ ounces) cream of mushroom soup

1 cup baby carrots, peeled

1 cup mushrooms, sliced

3 cups chicken stock

1 sprig of fresh thyme

Dumplings (see recipe on page 164)

1. Wash chicken and pat dry.
2. Season chicken with salt, pepper and poultry seasoning.
3. Pour oil into rice cooker and press COOK; heat oil for 5 minutes.
4. Place chicken into rice cooker and brown on both sides.
5. Add onions, celery, carrots and mushrooms; sauté for 1 minute.
6. Place remaining ingredients, except dumplings, into rice cooker; stir.
7. Secure lid and press COOK; cook for 45 minutes.
8. Prepare dumplings.
9. Spoon 6 mounds of dumpling batter over chicken.
10. Secure lid and press COOK; cook for an additional 5 minutes.

Deb's Tip:
To make preparation faster, cut up refrigerated biscuit dough and use them as dumplings.

Pork

SWEET CHERRY PEPPER PORK CHOPS

Ingredients:

2 tablespoons extra-virgin olive oil

4 pork chops, boneless

1 box (6 ounces) long-grain & wild rice

1 jar (6 ounces) sweet cherry peppers with juice

1 cup water

1 tablespoon salt

1. Pour oil into rice cooker and press COOK; heat oil for 5 minutes.
2. Add pork to rice cooker.
3. Secure lid and press COOK; cook for 7 minutes.
4. Turn chops and cook for an additional 8 minutes.
5. Add rice with seasoning pack and remaining ingredients to rice cooker.
6. Secure lid and press COOK.
7. Cooking is complete when rice cooker switches to KEEP WARM (about 25 minutes).

PASS ME THE PORK

Makes 4 to 6 servings

Ingredients:

2 pound pork tenderloin, cut into 1-inch slices

2 tablespoons extra-virgin olive oil

½ cup sweet orange marmalade

½ cup orange juice

½ cup beef stock

1 tablespoon cider vinegar

2 tablespoons honey

1 tablespoon Asian hot garlic sauce

1 teaspoon salt

1 teaspoon freshly ground pepper

1. Pour oil into rice cooker and press COOK; heat oil for 5 minutes.

2. Add pork, salt and pepper to rice cooker; brown on all sides.

3. Add orange juice and stock to rice cooker.

4. Secure lid and press COOK; cook for 20 minutes.

5. Add remaining ingredients to rice cooker.

6. Secure lid and press COOK; cook for an additional 5 minutes.

7. Serve over rice.

APPLE FENNEL PORK ROAST

Ingredients:

3 pound pork roast, boneless, cut into 2-inch pieces

12 fresh apple slices

2 fresh figs, halved

1 medium onion, sliced

4 cups chicken stock

¼ cup balsamic vinegar

1 teaspoon salt

1 teaspoon cumin seeds

1 teaspoon fennel seeds

½ teaspoon freshly ground pepper

1. Place all ingredients into rice cooker.
2. Secure lid and press COOK; cook for 2 hours.
3. Cooking is complete when pork is falling apart.

Deb's Tip:
Serve with my Brown Rice and Barley Pilaf, the
recipe is on page 20.

SWEET & SOUR PORK

Ingredients:

2 tablespoons soy sauce

2 tablespoons rice wine vinegar

1 pound lean pork, cut into thin strips

2 garlic cloves, minced

1 tablespoon freshly grated ginger

¼ cup purple onions, thinly sliced

1 red bell pepper, thinly sliced

1 package (⅞ ounce) sweet and sour sauce seasoning

2 tablespoons sweet and sour dipping sauce

2 tablespoons cornstarch

½ cup chicken stock

2 carrots, thinly sliced on the bias

1 can (8 ounces) diced pineapple, drained

¼ cup green onions, chopped

1. In a bowl, combine pork, soy sauce and vinegar; let marinate for 1 hour.
2. Transfer pork and marinade to rice cooker.
3. Secure lid and press COOK.
4. Cook until rice cooker switches to KEEP WARM (about 15 minutes); stir.
5. Add ginger, garlic, carrots, onions and peppers to rice cooker.
6. Secure lid and press COOK; cook for 5 minutes.
7. In a small bowl, combine sweet and sour sauce seasoning, stock and cornstarch; mix well.
8. Transfer sauce mixture to rice cooker; stir.
9. Secure lid and press COOK; cook for an additional 10 minutes.
10. Add pineapple and dipping sauce to rice cooker; stir.
11. Garnish with chopped green onions and serve with hot steaming rice.

BEER BRAISED BABY BACK RIBS

Makes 4 servings

Ingredients:

1 slab baby back ribs, cut into individual ribs

1 teaspoon barbecue rub

1 tablespoon extra-virgin olive oil

1 bottle (12 ounces) dark beer

1 cup chicken stock

½ cup barbecue sauce

1. Wash and pat dry ribs.
2. Season ribs with barbecue rub.
3. Pour oil into rice cooker and press COOK; heat oil for 5 minutes.
4. Place ribs into rice cooker and brown on all sides.
5. Add beer, stock and barbecue sauce to rice cooker.
6. Secure lid and press COOK; cook for 1 hour.

Deb's Tip:
To make this meal complete, load the steamer basket with four ears of corn during the last 10 minutes of cooking.

APPLE PORK MEDALLIONS

Makes 4 to 6 servings

Ingredients:

2 tablespoons extra-virgin olive oil

1 to 1½ pound pork tenderloin, cut into 1-inch pieces

4 medium apples, cubed

2 packets artificial sweetener

1 medium onion, diced

½ cup orange juice

½ package fajita seasoning mix

½ cup yellow bell peppers, diced

½ cup carrots, diced

1. Pour oil into rice cooker and press COOK; heat oil for 5 minutes.
2. Add pork to rice cooker; brown on all sides.
3. Add remaining ingredients to rice cooker; stir.
4. Secure lid and press COOK; cook for 30 minutes.

PORK CARNITAS

Ingredients:

2 pound pork butt or tenderloin, cut into 2-inch cubes

1 package fajita seasoning mix

¼ cup cilantro, chopped

2 cups beef stock

1 can (10½ ounces) Mexican tomatoes

1 cup Mexican cheese, shredded

8 romaine lettuce cups

1. Place pork, seasoning, stock and tomatoes into rice cooker.
2. Secure lid and press COOK; cook for 3 hours.
3. Place pork in center of each lettuce cup.
4. Sprinkle with cilantro and cheese.

Seafood & Fish

FISH TACOS

Ingredients:

½ cup water

1 pound fresh cod, grouper or snapper

2 tablespoons lime juice

1 tablespoon fresh cilantro, chopped

1 taco dinner kit

1 cup lettuce, shredded

2 green onions, chopped

Sour cream

1. Mix half the taco seasoning from the dinner kit with water and lime juice; pour into rice cooker.
2. Place fish into rice cooker; top with cilantro and half the package of taco sauce from the dinner kit.
3. Secure lid and press COOK; cook for 15 minutes.
4. Remove fish from rice cooker.
5. Heat taco shells according to package directions.
6. Place ¼ cup of fish into each taco shell; top with lettuce, sour cream and taco sauce.

Deb's Tip:
If you don't have fresh fish, just use frozen fish and add 5 minutes to the cooking time.

MARGARITA SHRIMP

Ingredients:

1 tablespoon extra-virgin olive oil

3 green onions, finely chopped

3 garlic cloves, minced

2 tablespoons fresh cilantro, chopped

1 small serrano pepper, chopped and seeds removed

1 cup bottled margarita mix

½ cup chicken stock

¼ cup orange juice

1 pound large shrimp, peeled and deveined

2 tablespoons salted butter

1. Place all ingredients, except shrimp and butter, into rice cooker.
2. Secure lid and press COOK; cook for 10 minutes.
3. Add shrimp and butter to rice cooker; stir.
4. Secure lid and press COOK; cook for 5 additional minutes.

Deb's Tip:
This dish is best served with my Green Rice, you can find the recipe on page 16.

EASY SHRIMP DIJON

Ingredients:

1 pound large shrimp, peeled and deveined

½ cup chicken stock

1 cup honey mustard dressing

½ cup cream

1 tablespoon fresh tarragon

1. Place all ingredients into rice cooker.
2. Secure lid and press COOK; cook for 15 minutes; stir.
3. If shrimp are not entirely cooked through, cook for an additional 5 minutes on KEEP WARM.

SHRIMP CREOLE

Ingredients:

1 tablespoon extra-virgin olive oil

1 medium onion, chopped

2 garlic cloves, minced

1 celery stalk, chopped

1 can (14½ ounces) tomatoes with green peppers

2 tablespoons fresh parsley, chopped

1 teaspoon seafood seasoning

1 bay leaf

1 pound large shrimp, peeled and deveined

¼ cup water

1. Pour oil into rice cooker and press COOK; heat oil for 5 minutes.

2. Add onions to rice cooker; cook for 5 minutes.

3. Add celery and garlic to rice cooker; stir and cook for 2 minutes.

4. Add shrimp, tomatoes, seasoning and bay leaf to rice cooker.

5. Secure lid and press COOK; cook for 20 minutes.

6. Discard bay leaf and serve over hot rice.

SPICY SHRIMP BOIL

Ingredients:

1 bottle (12 ounces) beer

½ cup vinegar

1 tablespoon pickling spice

2 tablespoons seafood seasoning

2 garlic cloves, minced

1 small onion, quartered

1 lemon, halved

1 pound large shrimp

1. Place all ingredients, except shrimp, into rice cooker.
2. Secure lid and press COOK; cook for 15 minutes.
3. Add shrimp to rice cooker; cook for 3 minutes; stir.
4. Unplug rice cooker.
5. Shrimp should be curled and pink.
6. Let shrimp sit for 10 minutes with the lid open.
7. Strain shrimp and serve on a cool platter.

Deb's Tip:
To make a great dipping sauce, just mix 1 tablespoon of
seafood seasoning with 2 tablespoons of vinegar.

CIOPPINO

Makes 6 to 8 servings

Ingredients:

2 tablespoons extra-virgin olive oil

1 medium onion, diced

3 garlic cloves, sliced

3 tablespoons tomato paste

1 teaspoon salt

½ teaspoon freshly ground pepper

1 cup chicken stock

1 can (14½ ounces) diced tomatoes with onions and green peppers

1 cup dry white wine

1 bay leaf

12 large sea scallops

5 ounces mild white fish

12 clams or mussels

6 crab claws

Fresh parsley, chopped

1. Pour oil into rice cooker and press COOK; heat oil for 5 minutes.
2. Add onions to rice cooker; cook for 3 minutes.
3. Add garlic to rice cooker; cook for an additional 1 minute.
4. Add tomato paste, salt and pepper to rice cooker; cook for 3 minutes.
5. Add chicken stock, wine, tomatoes and bay leaf to rice cooker; cook for 15 minutes.
6. Add seafood to rice cooker; stir.
7. Secure lid and press COOK; cook for 8 minutes.
8. Garnish with parsley.

Deb's Tip:
Dip some warm French bread into the delicious broth.

CLAM BAKE

Ingredients:

2 cups dry white wine

1 teaspoon salt

1 lemon, halved

5 peppercorns

4 small potatoes

1 large onion, quartered

1 to 1½ pound whole Maine lobster

2 ears of corn, husked

½ pound steamer clams

1. Place wine, salt and peppercorns into rice cooker.
2. Secure lid and press COOK; cook for 5 minutes.
3. Add potatoes and onions to rice cooker; cook for 15 minutes.
4. Place lobster head first into rice cooker and quickly secure the lid.
5. Press COOK; cook for 7 minutes.
6. Add clams and corn to rice cooker; cook for an additional 5 minutes.

Deb's Tip:
Don't forget the melted butter and nut crackers for cracking the claws.

134

POACHED SALMON

Ingredients:

1 tablespoon extra-virgin olive oil

2 garlic cloves, minced

1 cup chicken stock

1 cup dry white wine

1 lemon, thinly sliced

1 sprig of fresh dill

1 teaspoon salt

4 whole peppercorns

4 salmon steaks, 1-inch thick

1. Pour oil into rice cooker and press COOK; heat oil for 5 minutes.
2. Add garlic to rice cooker.
3. Secure lid and press COOK; cook for 3 minutes.
4. Add stock, wine, lemon, dill, salt and peppercorns to rice cooker; cook for 5 minutes.
5. Add salmon to rice cooker; cook for an additional 12 minutes.

Deb's Tip:
For a delicious sauce to compliment this meal, take a half cup of sour cream, 1 tablespoon chopped parsley, 1 teaspoon lemon juice and 1 teaspoon dry ranch seasoning; mix and serve with the salmon.

ROSEMARY GARLIC & TILAPIA

By Shannon Dillman   Makes 3 to 6 servings

Ingredients:

3 frozen tilapia filets

4 cups basmati rice

6 cups water

1 tablespoon coconut oil

4 tablespoons garlic-rosemary seasoning

1 bag (12 ounces) frozen corn

1. Place rice, oil, water, seasoning and corn into rice cooker.
2. Fit rice cooker with steamer basket and place tilapia into basket.
3. Secure lid and press COOK.
4. Cook until rice cooker switches to KEEP WARM (about 20 minutes).
5. Shred tilapia with fork, toss with rice and serve.

PAELLA

Ingredients:

1 cup Arborio rice

1 cup chicken stock

1 small onion, chopped

1 garlic clove, minced

18 strands saffron

Pinch of freshly ground pepper

Pinch of ground red pepper

¼ cup tender young peas, fresh or frozen

6 stuffed green olives, sliced

2 tablespoons fresh parsley, chopped

¾ cup white wine

12 large shrimp, peeled and deveined

12 small clams, scrubbed

12 black mussels

1. Place all ingredients, except seafood and wine, into rice cooker.
2. Secure lid and press COOK; cook for 20 minutes.
3. Add seafood and wine to rice cooker; cook for an additional 10 minutes.
4. Stir well and serve.

SNAPPY VERA CRUZ

Ingredients:

½ cup chicken stock

1 to 1½ pounds snapper filets

1 cup salsa

1 can (10½ ounces) Mexican tomatoes with lime juice and cilantro

2 tablespoons capers

2 tablespoons sliced green olives

1. Place all ingredients into rice cooker.
2. Secure lid and press COOK; cook for 15 minutes.
3. Serve with hot rice.

Breads & Sweets

APPLE CRISP

Makes 6 to 8 servings

Ingredients:

2½ pounds tart apples, peeled and cored, thinly sliced

½ cup sugar

1 teaspoon cinnamon

½ teaspoon Chinese five-spice powder

6 tablespoons unsalted butter

1 container (9 ounces) apple crisp mix

1. In a bowl, toss apples with sugar, cinnamon and five-spice powder.
2. Transfer apples to rice cooker.
3. Using a food processor fitted with a chopping blade, combine butter and crisp mix; sprinkle over apples.
4. Secure lid and press COOK.
5. When rice cooker switches to KEEP WARM (about 10 minutes), press COOK again.
6. Cooking is complete when rice cooker switches to KEEP WARM (about 5 minutes).

Deb's Tip:
Serve with rum-raisin ice cream.

SIMPLY FABULOUS MILK CHOCOLATE FUDGE

Makes 16 servings

Ingredients:

24 ounces milk chocolate morsels

1 can (14 ounces) sweetened condensed milk

1 cup whole pecans

1 teaspoon extract (vanilla, rum or peppermint)

Butter-flavored non-stick cooking spray

1. Place morsels into rice cooker.
2. Secure lid and set rice cooker to KEEP WARM; cook for 15 minutes.
3. Stir chocolate until smooth.
4. If any unmelted morsels remain, cook for an additional 5 minutes on KEEP WARM.
5. Add pecans, milk and extract to rice cooker; stir.
6. Secure lid and set rice cooker to KEEP WARM; cook for 10 minutes.
7. Spray a 9 X 9 baking dish with non-stick spray.
8. Transfer fudge mixture to baking dish; cover with plastic wrap.
9. Refrigerate for 2 hours; cut fudge into 1-inch squares.

Deb's Tip:
Try using white chocolate morsels instead of milk chocolate.

COOKIES & CREAM BARS

Ingredients:

24 chocolate cream filled cookies

2 tablespoons unsalted butter

8 ounces cream cheese

1 can (14 ounces) sweetened condensed milk

1. Using a food processor, crush cookies.
2. Remove 1 cup of crushed cookies from food processor; set aside.
3. Add butter to food processor and blend until crumbled.
4. Press the butter-cookie mixture into the bottom of the rice cooker.
5. Using a food processor, mix cream cheese and milk.
6. Transfer cream cheese mixture to rice cooker and sprinkle with remaining crushed cookies.
7. Secure lid and press COOK; cook for 10 minutes.
8. Press COOK again; cook for an additional 10 minutes.
9. Set rice cooker to KEEP WARM and cook for 25 minutes.
10. Invert onto cake stand.
11. Flip over and cut into 1-inch bars.

MOIST CHOCOLATE CAKE

Ingredients:

1 box (18½ ounces) devil's food cake mix

1 cup mayonnaise

1½ cups milk

1. Using a food processor, combine all ingredients; mix until smooth.
2. Spray rice cooker with non-stick spray.
3. Pour mixture into rice cooker.
4. Secure lid and press COOK; cook for 1 hour.
5. Rice cooker will switch to KEEP WARM multiple times during the 1 hour, press COOK every 10 minutes.
6. Test cake for doneness by inserting a toothpick into the center. If it comes out clean, cake is done.
7. Unplug rice cooker and let rest for 30 minutes; invert onto a plate and let cool.
8. Frost cake.

Deb's Tip:
To give this cake a little punch, add a couple tablespoons of hazelnut liqueur.

PUMPKIN PIE

Ingredients:

½ cup pecans

12 ginger snap cookies

2 tablespoons salted butter

3 tablespoons brown sugar

2 large eggs

1 cup heavy cream

1 can (15 ounces) pumpkin purée

1 teaspoon pumpkin spice

1 teaspoon vanilla

½ teaspoon salt

½ cup sugar

1. Using a food processor, chop ginger snaps, pecans, butter and brown sugar until finely crumbled.
2. Spray rice cooker with non-stick spray.
3. Press cookie mixture into the bottom of the rice cooker.
4. Secure lid and press COOK; cook for 5 minutes.
5. Using a mixer, combine eggs, cream, pumpkin purée, spice, vanilla, salt and pepper; blend until smooth.
6. Pour pumpkin mixture into rice cooker over the cookie mixture; sprinkle lightly with additional pumpkin spice.
7. Secure lid and press COOK; cook for 30 minutes.
8. Rice cooker will switch to KEEP WARM multiple times during the 30 minutes, press COOK every 10 minutes.
9. Set rice cooker to KEEP WARM and cook for an additional 30 minutes.
10. Unplug rice cooker and let rest for 1 hour.
11. Run a butter knife around the edge of the pie and invert onto a plate; quickly flip onto another plate.
12. Cover and chill until ready to serve.

LEMON POPPY SEED BREAD

By Bonnie Davis   Makes 10 to 12 servings

Ingredients:

1 box (18¼ ounces) lemon cake mix
1 box (3 ounces) instant lemon pudding
4 large eggs
½ cup vegetable oil
1 cup water
¼ cup poppy seeds

1. Using a food processor, combine all ingredients; mix well.
2. Spray rice cooker with non-stick spray.
3. Pour mixture into rice cooker.
4. Secure lid and press COOK; cook for 1 hour.
5. Rice cooker will switch to KEEP WARM multiple times during the 1 hour, press COOK every 20 minutes.
6. Test bread for doneness by inserting a toothpick into the center. If it comes out clean, bread is done.
7. Unplug rice cooker and let rest for 30 minutes; invert bread onto a plate.
8. Cover until ready to serve.

Bonnie's Tip:
This bread is so delicious with raspberry jam.

SPICED POACHED PEARS

Ingredients:

3 pears

3 cups cranberry juice

½ cup sugar

2 whole cloves

1 sprig of rosemary

1 orange zest, 6-inches long, julienned

1. Using a melon baller, core pears from the bottom and peel them, leaving the stems intact.
2. Place pears on their sides into rice cooker.
3. Add remaining ingredients to rice cooker.
4. Secure lid and press COOK; cook for 20 minutes.
5. Transfer pears to freezer.
6. Continue to cook sauce until it is reduced to 1½ cups.
7. Transfer sauce to a metal bowl set in a larger bowl filled with ice; stir sauce until cool.
8. Serve pears in a shallow dish with sauce and garnish with orange strips.

Deb's Tip:
You can substitute your favorite red wine for the cranberry juice.

CHERRY FUDGE CAKE

By D'Ann Mathews   Makes 8 to 10 servings

Ingredients:

1 cup flour

1 cup sugar

½ cup unsweetened cocoa powder

1 teaspoon baking soda

½ teaspoon baking powder

¼ teaspoon salt

1 egg

½ cup coffee

½ cup maraschino cherry juice

¼ cup canola oil

1 teaspoon vanilla extract

1 cup maraschino cherries, halved

Non-stick cooking spray

1. In a bowl, combine flour, sugar, cocoa powder, baking soda, baking powder and salt; mix well.
2. Add oil, egg, cherry juice, coffee and vanilla to bowl; mix until batter is smooth.
3. Spray rice cooker with non-stick spray.
4. Place cherries into rice cooker and pour batter over cherries.
5. Secure lid and press COOK; cook for 75 minutes.

SIMPLE & DELICIOUS CORN CAKE

Ingredients:

3 tablespoons unsalted butter

2 boxes (8½ ounces each) corn muffin mix

¾ cup milk

2 large eggs

1. In a bowl, combine all ingredients, except butter; mix well.
2. Place butter into rice cooker and press COOK.
3. When butter is melted, pour batter into rice cooker.
4. Secure lid and press COOK; cook for 45 minutes.

BLUEBERRY LEMON UPSIDE DOWN CAKE

Ingredients:

Non-stick cooking spray

12 ounces frozen blueberries

1 tablespoon lemon juice

½ cup sugar

1 box (10¼ ounces) lemon supreme cake mix

1 box (3.4 ounces) instant lemon pudding mix

4 large eggs

1 cup water

⅓ cup vegetable oil

1. Spray rice cooker with non-stick spray.
2. In a bowl, combine blueberries, lemon juice and sugar; mix well.
3. Using a mixer, combine cake mix, pudding mix, eggs, oil and water; blend until smooth.
4. Place blueberries into rice cooker and top with cake mixture.
5. Secure lid and press COOK; cook for 30 minutes.
6. Rice cooker will switch to KEEP WARM during the 30 minutes, press COOK every 10 minutes.
7. Set rice cooker to KEEP WARM and cook for an additional 30 minutes.
8. Invert cake onto a cake stand and serve.

Deb's Tip:
For a twist, try substituting strawberry or vanilla cake mix for the lemon cake mix.

CARAMEL FOR APPLES

Makes 5 servings

Ingredients:

1 bag (14 ounces) caramels

2 teaspoons water

5 medium apples

5 wooden sticks

1. Place caramels and water into rice cooker.
2. Secure lid and press COOK; cook for 45 minutes; stir occasionally.
3. Insert sticks into apples and dip into caramel sauce until covered.
4. Place apples onto a sheet of parchment paper to cool.

Deb's Tip:
Roll apples into your favorite candy while the caramel is still warm.

PINA COLADA RICE PUDDING

By Christina Chancey   Makes 6 to 8 servings

Ingredients:

2 cups white rice

2 cups water

1 can (12 ounces) pina colada mix

½ cup pineapple chunks with juice

1 cup heavy cream

1. Rinse rice.
2. Place rice and water into rice cooker.
3. Secure lid and press COOK; cook for 20 minutes.
4. Add pina colada mix, cream and pineapple chunks to rice cooker.
5. Secure lid and press COOK; cook for an additional 10 minutes.
6. For a softer consistency, add ½ cup of cream and stir.

Christina's Tip:
For some extra flavor, add some rum to this recipe.

BLUEBERRY MUFFIN BREAD PUDDING

Makes 6 to 8 servings

Ingredients:

8 large blueberry muffins

1 box (5½ ounces) flan mix with caramel sauce

4 cups milk

1. In a bowl, combine flan mix and milk; stir.

2. Pour mixture into rice cooker.

3. Break apart muffins and drop into rice cooker.

4. Secure lid and press COOK.

5. Cooking is complete when rice cooker switches to KEEP WARM (about 45 minutes).

Deb's Tip:
Top bread pudding with the caramel sauce that comes with the flan mix.

CARAMEL PEANUT BUTTER CEREAL TREATS

Makes 12 servings

Ingredients:

1 bag (14 ounces) caramels

1 bag (10 ounces) mini marshmallows

10 cups crispy rice cereal, plain or chocolate

½ cup peanut butter

Butter-flavored non-stick cooking spray

1. Place all ingredients into rice cooker.
2. Secure lid and press COOK; cook for 45 minutes; stir occasionally.
3. Spray a 9 X 13 baking dish with non-stick spray.
4. Pour mixture into baking dish; let cool for 30 minutes.
5. Cut into squares.

DUMPLINGS

Ingredients:

1 cup all-purpose flour

½ teaspoon salt

1 tablespoon baking powder

2 tablespoons shortening

½ cup buttermilk

1 tablespoon fresh parsley, chopped

1. In a bowl, combine flour, salt and baking powder.

2. Add shortening and parsley to bowl; mixture will look like crumbs.

3. Add buttermilk and stir until moist.

For more of Deb's delicious ideas, please visit:

www.cookingwithdeb.com

INDEX

INDEX

INDEX

INDEX

INDEX

5-CUP RICE COOKER CONVERSIONS

RICE COOKER JAMBALAYA

1/2 cup New Orleans style jambalaya mix
1 1/4 cup chicken stock
1 tablespoon extra-virgin olive oil
1/4 pound kielbasa
1/4 pound shrimp
1/4 pound cooked chicken
1 cup tomatoes, chopped
1 tablespoon onions, chopped
1 tablespoon green peppers, chopped
2/3 cup frozen corn
1 cup black beans, drained

EASY FIESTA RICE

1/4 cup onions, chopped
1 can (10oz) diced tomatoes with lime juice and cilantro, drained
1 cup long-grain rice
3/4 cup chicken stock
1/2 teaspoon salt
Pinch of freshly ground pepper

DEB'S FAVORITE FRIED RICE

1 1/2 teaspoons sesame oil
1 garlic clove, minced
1/2 teaspoon freshly grated ginger
1/4 teaspoon sugar
1 small carrot, shredded
2 cups long-grain rice, cooked
1/4 cup chicken, cut in 1/2-inch pieces
1 tablespoon soy sauce
1 teaspoon fish sauce
1 tablespoon green onions, chopped
1/4 cup bean sprouts
1/4 cup peas
1 large egg, beaten

BROWN RICE WITH WHITE MISO

1 1/2 cups long-grain brown rice
3 cups water
2 teaspoons white miso paste

RISOTTO WITH ASPARAGUS

1 cup Arborio rice
5oz fresh asparagus, peeled cut into
1-inch pieces
1/4 cup onions, chopped
1 1/2 tablespoons salted butter, melted
1/2 teaspoon salt
1/4 teaspoon freshly ground pepper
2 cups chicken stock
1/2 cup Parmesan cheese, grated

CUBAN STYLE BLACK BEANS

1 cup dry black beans
1 envelope Spanish seasoning
3 cups beef stock
1/4 cup onions, diced
1/4 cup red bell peppers, chopped
1 1/2 teaspoons cilantro, chopped
1 ripe plum tomato, chopped
1 garlic clove, minced
3/4 cup canned tomatoes with green chiles and lime

RED BEANS & RICE

1 cup long-grain rice
1/2 cup red beans, canned or cooked, drained
1 celery stalk, chopped
1/2 cup onions, chopped
1 garlic clove, minced
1/4 cup ham, diced
1/4 cup smoked sausage, sliced
1 cup beef stock
1/2 teaspoon hot sauce
1/2 teaspoon Worchestershire sauce
1/4 cup tomato sauce
1/2 teaspoon prepared mustard
1 small bay leaf
1/2 teaspoon Cajun spice

NEW ENGLAND BAKED BEANS

1/2 pound navy beans
3 ounces Salt pork, cut in 1-inch pieces
1/2 cup onions, chopped
2 cups water
1/4 teaspoon baking soda
1/4 cup sugar
2 tablespoons molasses
1 1/2 teaspoons prepared mustard
1 1/2 teaspoons salt
2 tablespoons maple syrup
1 1/2 teaspoons Jamaican pepper sauce
1 slice fresh ginger

HUMMUS

1 cup dry garbonzo beans
3 1/2 cups water
2 whole garlic cloves
3 cups chicken stock
1 1/2 tablespoons tahini
1 tablespoon fresh lemon juice
1 1/2 teaspoons extra-virgin olive oil
Pinch of cayenne pepper
1 teaspoon salt

ITALIAN POLENTA

2 cups water
1/2 cup coarse grain yellow polenta
1/2 teaspoon salt
1/4 teaspoon freshly ground pepper
1/4 cup unsalted butter
1/4 cup Parmesan cheese, grated

GARLIC MASHED POTATOES

3 Yukon gold potatoes, peeled and halved
1 cup chicken stock
1/4 cup heavy cream
2 small garlic cloves
1/2 teaspoon salt
1/4 teaspoon freshly ground pepper

SCALLOPED POTATOES WITH CHEDDAR CHEESE

1 tablespoon unsalted butter
1/4 cup onions, thinly sliced
1 garlic clove, minced
1 pound Russet potatoes, peeled, sliced
1/8-inch thick
1 1/2 teaspoons fresh thyme leaves
1/2 teaspoon kosher salt
1/4 teaspoon freshly ground pepper
1/2 cup chicken stock
1/4 cup heavy cream
Pinch of nutmeg
1/4 cup Cheddar cheese, shredded
1 tablespoon fresh chives, chopped

EGGPLANT LASAGNA

1 small eggplant, sliced into 1/4-inch rounds
1 large egg, beaten
1 1/2 tablespoons extra-virgin olive oil
1 cup whole milk Ricotta cheese
2 tablespoons Parmesan cheese, shredded
1/2 teaspoon salt
1/4 teaspoon freshly ground pepper
2 cups pasta sauce
1 cup Mozzarella cheese, shredded
3 basil leaves, torn

BONNIE'S CHEESY RICE & VEGGIES

1 cup basmati or long-grain rice
1 1/4 cups chicken stock
1 cup onions, finely chopped
1/2 cup celery, sliced
1 cup frozen broccoli
1 cup frozen cauliflower
1/2 cup cream of mushroom soup
1/2 cup pasteurized process cheese sauce
1/4 cup milk
2 tablespoons salted butter

5-CUP RICE COOKER CONVERSIONS

GREEK LEMON CHICKEN SOUP

2 skinless chicken breasts, diced
1/2 cup onions, chopped
1/2 cup fresh spinach, chopped
3 cups chicken stock
1/4 cup orzo pasta
2 tablespoons fresh lemon juice
1/2 teaspoon kosher salt
1/4 teaspoon freshly ground pepper
2 teaspoons fresh mint leaves, chopped
1 large egg, beaten

VEGETABLE SOUP WITH PASTA

1/2 cup onions, chopped
2 teaspoons extra-virgin olive oil
1 garlic clove, minced
1/2 cup celery, sliced
1/2 cup carrots, sliced
1/2 cup cabbage, sliced
1 cup canned diced tomatoes with oregano and garlic
3 cups vegetable stock
1 sprig of fresh thyme
1/2 cup wagon wheel pasta

CLAM CHOWDER

12 steamer or littleneck clams
1/2 cup water
1/4 cup onions, chopped
1/4 cup celery root, diced
1/4 teaspoon freshly ground pepper
2 ounces salt pork, rind removed, cut into 1/4-inch pieces
1 sprig of fresh thyme
1/2 teaspoon salt
1 cup chicken stock
3/4 cup cream
Fresh parsley, chopped

SPLIT PEA SOUP

1 cup dried split peas
1/2 cup ham, diced
2 carrots, cut into 2-inch pieces
1/2 cup onions, diced
2 celery stalks, cut into 1-inch pieces
1 garlic clove, minced
1 bay leaf
1 sprig of fresh thyme
3 cups chicken stock
1/4 teaspoon freshly ground pepper

THAI STYLE CHICKEN SOUP

1 1/2 teaspoons extra-virgin olive oil
1/4 cup purple onions, thinly sliced
1/4 cup red bell peppers, julienned
1 garlic clove, minced
1/2 teaspoon freshly grated ginger
1/3 cup bamboo shoots
1 tablespoon creamy peanut butter
1 cup cooked chicken, shredded
1 cup coconut milk
1 cup chicken stock
1/2 teaspoon Chinese five-spice powder
1 1/2 teaspoons fish sauce
1 small lemon, juice and zest
1 tablespoon green onions, chopped
1 tablespoon cilantro, chopped

BORSCHT

1 1/2 teaspoons extra-virgin olive oil
1/2 cup onions, diced
1/4 cup carrots, diced
1/4 cup celery, diced
1/4 cup cabbage, shredded
1/2 cup potatoes, diced
1 cup beef stock
1cup beets, peeled and diced
1 cup petite diced tomatoes
1/2 teaspoon cider vinegar
1/2 teaspoon salt
1/4 teaspoon freshly ground pepper
Sour cream
4 sprigs of fresh dill

ALMOST HOMEMADE CHICKEN SOUP

1 boneless, skinless frozen chicken breast
3 cups chicken stock
1 sprig of fresh thyme
1/4 cup carrots, sliced 1-inch thick
1/4 cup onions, diced
1/2 teaspoon salt
1/4 teaspoon freshly ground pepper
1/4 cup wide egg noodles
1 1/2 teaspoons fresh parsley, chopped

BUTTERNUT SQUASH-APPLE SOUP

1 1/2 teaspoons extra-virgin olive oil
1/4 cup onions, chopped
1 small butternut squash, peeled and seeded
1 Granny Smith apple, peeled and cored
1 1/2 cups chicken stock
1 cup apple cider
1 sprig of fresh thyme
1 sprig of fresh rosemary
1 sage leave
1/4 cup cream
Sour cream

ROASTED RED PEPPER SOUP

1 tablespoon extra-virgin olive oil
3 garlic cloves, chopped
1/2 cup onions, chopped
1/2 cup celery, chopped
1/2 cup carrots, chopped
1 tablespoon tomato paste
2 cups roasted red peppers, drained
3 cups vegetable stock
1 bay leaf
1/2 teaspoon salt
1/4 teaspoon freshly ground pepper
Fresh basil, chopped
Sour cream

BEEF BARLEY SOUP

1 pound beef shank, bone-in
2 teaspoons extra-virgin olive oil
1 1/3 cup dry red wine
3/4 teaspoon salt
1/4 teaspoon freshly ground pepper
1/2 small onion, quartered
2 1/2 cups beef stock
2 carrots, sliced
1 celery stalk, sliced
1/2 cup onions, thinly sliced
1 cup petite diced tomatoes
1 sprig of fresh thyme
1 bay leaf
1/3 cup pearl barley

CREAMY ONE POT MACARONI AND CHEESE

1 cup elbow macaroni
1 cup chicken stock
1/2 teaspoon salt
1/2 teaspoon freshly ground pepper
1/2 cup cream
3/4 cup mild Cheddar cheese, shredded
1/4 cup Mozzarella cheese, shredded
1 tablespoon salted butter
Pinch of nutmeg

5-CUP RICE COOKER CONVERSIONS

LINGUINI & LENTILS

1 cup lentils
1 1/2 teaspoons extra virgin olive oil
1 garlic clove, minced
1/2 cup onions, chopped
1 carrot, chopped
5 cups water
2 tablespoons tomato sauce
1/2 teaspoon salt
1/4 teaspoon freshly ground pepper
Pinch crushed red pepper flakes
3 ounces dry linguini nest

BAKED ZITI

1/2 pound ground beef
1/4 cup onions, chopped
1 garlic clove, minced
1/2 teaspoon salt
1/4 teaspoon freshly ground pepper
1 cup dry ziti pasta
1 cup beef stock
2 cups pasta sauce
1 cup whole milk Ricotta cheese
1 cup Mozzarella cheese, shredded
1/4 cup Parmesan cheese, shredded

PASTA FAGIOLI

1 garlic clove, minced
1/4 cup pepperoni, skin removed, diced
1 1/2 teaspoons extra-virgin olive oil
1 cup cannellini beans
1/2 cup tomato sauce
3 cups water
1/4 teaspoon freshly ground pepper
1/2 teaspoon salt
Pinch crushed red pepper flakes
1 cup ditalini pasta

ORECCHIETTE WITH BROCCOLI AND SAUSAGE

1/2 pound Italian turkey sausage, casings removed
2 garlic cloves, sliced
1 cup orecchiette pasta
1 1/2 cups chicken stock
1 cup broccoli flowerets
Pinch crushed red pepper flakes
1/2 cup Parmesan cheese, shredded
Fresh parsley, chopped

PAD THAI

1 garlic clove, minced
1/2 teaspoon sesame oil
1 box Pad Thai stir-fry rice noodles with sauce
2 cups water
1 tablespoon lime juice
1/2 cup bean sprouts
1/2 pound medium shrimp, peeled and deveined
2 green onions, cut into 1-inch pieces
1 1/2 teaspoons fresh cilantro, chopped
1/4 cup peanuts
1/4 teaspoon crushed red pepper flakes

PASTA BOWS WITH PROSCIUTTO AND PEAS

1 1/2 teaspoons extra-virgin olive oil
2 small garlic cloves, minced
2 ounces prosciutto, chopped into 1/4-inch pieces
1 cup dry bow tie pasta
1 cup chicken stock
3/4 cup tiny peas
1/4 cup dry white wine
1/4 cup cream
1/4 teaspoon salt
1/4 teaspoon freshly ground pepper
3 mint or basil leaves, chopped

TUSCAN SHRIMP PASTA

1 cup dry ziti or penne
1 cup chicken stock
1/4 cup purple onions, thinly sliced
1 garlic clove, minced
1 cup artichoke hearts, drained and quartered
2 tablespoons sun-dried tomatoes, oil-packed
1/2 pound shrimp, peeled and deveined
2 tablespoons Kalamata olives
1/4 cup fresh pesto

STUFFED PEPPERS

1/2 pound ground beef
1/4 cup onions, chopped
2 bell peppers
1/2 cup rice, cooked
1 cup canned diced tomatoes with basil, garlic and oregano
1/2 teaspoon salt
1/4 teaspoon freshly ground pepper
1 cup pasta sauce
2 slices Swiss cheese

RICE COOKER MEATBALLS

1 1/2 teaspoons extra-virgin olive oil
1/2 cup onions, minced
2 garlic cloves, minced
1 pound ground beef
1/2 cup bread crumbs, finely grated
1/4 cup beef stock
1/4 cup Parmesan cheese, grated
1/2 teaspoon garlic salt
1/4 teaspoon freshly ground pepper
1 large egg, beaten
2 cups tomato sauce

CORNED BEEF AND CABBAGE

1 pound corned beef brisket, cut in half
1 bottle (12 ounces) dark beer
1 1/2 cups beef stock
2 garlic cloves, minced
1 medium onion, quartered
1 tablespoon pickling spice
2 medium red potatoes, halved
1/2 cabbage head, cut into wedges
1/2 cup baby carrots

SLOPPY JOES

1 pound lean ground beef
1/2 cup onions, chopped
1 garlic clove, minced
1/2 cup green bell peppers, chopped
1 1/2 tablespoons Worchestershire sauce
1 1/2 tablespoons brown sugar
1 teaspoon yellow mustard
1 teaspoon cider vinegar
1 teaspoon chili powder
1/3 cup tomato paste
1/2 cup water

CHICKEN ENCHILADA CASSEROLE

1 cup cooked chicken
1/4 cup chopped green chiles
1/2 package taco seasoning
1/2 cup chicken stock
1 1/3 cup tortilla soup
Tortilla chips
2/3 cup enchilada sauce
1/2 cup mild Cheddar cheese, shredded
2 green onions, chopped
Sour cream

CHICKEN CACCIATORE

4 boneless, skinless frozen chicken tenderloins
Pinch of garlic and herb seasoning
Pinch of Italian seasoning
1/2 teaspoon sugar
1/2 cup onions, thinly sliced
1/4 cup red wine
1/2 cup mushrooms, thinly sliced
3/4 cup spaghetti sauce
1/2 cup four-cheese mix, shredded

5-CUP RICE COOKER CONVERSIONS

CHICKEN AND YELLOW RICE WITH PEAS

1 cup yellow rice
1/2 cup cooked chicken
1 tablespoon extra-virgin olive oil
1/4 cup onions, copped
1 garlic clove, minced
1/4 cup red bell peppers, cut into strips
1/2 cup frozen peas
1 tablespoon stuffed green olives, sliced
2 cups chicken stock

CHICKEN AND DUMPLINGS

4 medium chicken thighs or legs, skinless
1/2 teaspoon salt
Pinch of poultry seasoning
1/4 teaspoon freshly ground pepper
1/2 teaspoon extra-virgin olive oil
1/2 cup onions, sliced
1/2 cup celery, diced
3/4 cup cream of mushroom soup
1/2 cup baby carrots, peeled
1/2 cup mushrooms, sliced
1 1/2 cups chickens stock
1 sprig of fresh thyme
Dumplings (see recipe on page 164)

APPLE FENNEL PORK ROAST

1 1/2 pound pork roast, boneless, cut into 2-inch pieces
6 fresh apple slices
1 fresh fig, halved
1/2 cup onions, sliced
2 cups chicken stock
2 tablespoons balsamic vinegar
1/2 teaspoon salt
1/2 teaspoon cumin seeds
1/2 teaspoon fennel seeds
1/4 teaspoon freshly ground pepper

CIOPPINO

1 tablespoon extra-virgin olive oil
1/2 cup onions, diced
2 garlic cloves, sliced
1 1/2 tablespoons tomato paste
1/2 teaspoon salt
1/4 teaspoon freshly ground pepper
1/2 cup chicken stock
1 cup canned diced tomatoes with onions and green peppers
1/2 cup dry white wine
1 bay leaf
6 large sea scallops
3 ounces mild white fish
6 clams or mussels
6 crab claws
Fresh parsley, chopped

CLAM BAKE

1 1/2 cups dry white wine
3/4 teaspoon salt
1 lemon, halved
3 peppercorns
2 small potatoes
1/2 large onion, quartered
1 pound whole Maine lobster
1 ear of corn, husked
1/3 pound steamer clams

ROSEMARY GARLIC AND TILAPIA

2 frozen tilapia filets
2 cups basmati rice
3 cups water
2 teaspoons coconut oil
2 tablespoons garlic-rosemary seasoning
3/4 cup frozen corn

MOIST CHOCOLATE CAKE

1 1/2 cups devil's food cake mix
1/2 cup mayonnaise
1 1/2 cups milk

LEMON POPPY SEED BREAD

1 1/2 cups lemon cake mix
1/4 cup instant lemon pudding
2 large eggs
1/4 cup vegetable oil
2/3 cup water
2 tablespoons poppy seeds

SPICED POACHED PAIRS

2 pears
3 cups cranberry juice
1/2 cup sugar
2 whole cloves
1 sprig of rosemary
1 orange zest, 6-inches long, julienned

CHERRY FUDGE CAKE

1/2 cup flour
1/2 cup sugar
1/4 cup unsweetened cocoa powder
1/2 teaspoon baking soda
1/4 teaspoon baking powder
Pinch of salt
1 egg yolk
1/4 cup coffee
1/4 cup maraschino cherry juice
2 tablespoons canola oil
1/2 teaspoon vanilla extract
1/2 cup maraschino cherries, halved
Non-stick cooking spray

BLUEBERRY MUFFIN BREAD PUDDING

4 large blueberry muffins
1/3 cup flan mix with caramel sauce
2 cups milk

CARAMEL PEANUT BUTTER CEREAL TREATS

1 cup caramels
3/4 cup mini marshmallows
5 cups crispy rice cereal
1/4 cup peanut butter
Butter-flavored non-stick cooking spray